Here's
The Deal

HERE'S THE DEAL

EVERYTHING YOU WISH A LAWYER WOULD TELL YOU ABOUT BUYING A SMALL BUSINESS

Joel Ankney

Copyright © 2017 by Joel Ankney. All rights reserved.

ISBN: 1539850811
ISBN 13: 9781539850816
Library of Congress Control Number: 2016918345
CreateSpace Independent Publishing Platform
North Charleston, South Carolina

Dedication

This is my first book.
All that I have accomplished is because Jenny believes in me.

Table of Contents

Acknowledgments · xv

About the Author · xvii

Preface · xix

I Am Not Your Lawyer Because You Read
this Book · xxi

Introduction · xxiii

Chapter 1	Evaluate Yourself First. · 1	
	Should I Own a Business? · · · · · · · · · · · · · · · · · · · 1	
	Should I Own This Business? · · · · · · · · · · · · · · 3	
Chapter 2	Assemble Your Team. · 7	
	Assemble Your Team at the Beginning of the Deal · 7	
	Who Should Be On Your Team? · · · · · · · · · · · · · 8	
	Close Confidant. · 8	
	Business Lawyer. · 10	
	Accountant. · 14	

	Business Broker	16
	Banker or Loan Officer	18
	How to Find Team Members	18
	Get Your Team in Place Early	20
Chapter 3	Finding Your Target	21
	Employee Purchase	21
	Financially Struggling Businesses	22
	Owner Aging Out	22
	Competitors	22
	Customers	23
	Word of Mouth	23
	Listings	23
	Brokers	24
	Franchises	24
Chapter 4	Valuing the Target Business	26
Chapter 5	Prepare for Hidden Costs	30
	Lender Financing Costs	31
	Raising Capital	32
	Professional Fees	32
	Retainers	34
	Pay-As-You-Go	34
	Defer to Closing	34
	Negotiate	35
	Inspection Costs	35
	Valuation Expert	35
	Environmental Assessment	36
	HVAC and Renovation Inspections	37
	Equipment and Machinery Inspections	38
	Prorated Expenses & Taxes	38

	Security Deposit 38
	Consent Fees 39
	Licenses and Government Approvals 39
	Insurance 40
	Broker's Commission 40
	Seller-Paid Closing Costs 41
Chapter 6	Financing the Purchase 42
	Your Own Cash 42
	Investors 42
	Private Placement 43
	Founder's Exemption 46
	Crowdfunding 47
	Pros and Cons of Investors 48
	Loan 51
	Bank Loan 51
	Small Business Administration Loan 52
	Line of Credit 53
	Second Mortgage 53
	Private Lender (Family or Friend) 54
	Angel Lender 54
	Hard Money Lender 55
	Cash Advance 55
	Retirement Benefits 56
	Seller-Financing 57
	Combinations 58
Chapter 7	What are You Buying? 60
	Equity Deal 60
	Asset Deal 62
	Real Estate 63
	Liabilities 64

Chapter 8	Before You Sign the Purchase Agreement	66
	Ask Probing Preliminary Questions	66
	Visit the Business	68
	Negotiate Significant Terms	69
	Letter of Intent	70
	Confidentiality or Nondisclosure Agreement	72
Chapter 9	Is it a Good Deal?	74
	Lien and Judgment Search	75
	Financial Information	76
	Significant Contracts	76
	Employees and Independent Contractors	78
	Equipment	79
	Environmental Issues	79
	Intellectual Property	80
Chapter 10	Purchase Agreement Drafting Problems	83
	Bad Templates—One-Size-Fits-All Forms	84
	Ambiguity	87
	Undefined Words	88
	Agreements to Agree	89
	Verbal Agreements Not in the Contract	90
Chapter 11	Anatomy of a Purchase Agreement	92
	The Parties	94
	Recitals or Purpose	95
	Purchased Assets	95
	Excluded Assets	96
	Purchase Price	96
	Payment Terms	99
	Allocation of Purchase Price	101
	Due Diligence or Inspection Period; Right to Terminate	102
	Financing Contingency	104

Assignment and Assumption of Contracts...105
Assignment and Assumption of Lease
or New Lease............................106
No Assumption (or Limited Assumption)
of Seller's Liabilities....................108
Prorations..............................108
Prepaids, Customer Deposits.............109
Post-Closing Transition..................110
Representations and Warranties..........111
    Representations and Warranties Made
    by Both Parties........................112
        Due Organization..................112
        Due Execution.....................112
        No Conflicts......................112
        Brokers...........................113
    Representations and Warranties Made
    by the Seller..........................113
        Title to Assets....................114
        Condition of Assets................114
        No Claims.........................114
        No Breach of Contracts and Leases..115
        Taxes.............................115
        Compliance with Law...............116
        Complete and True Information....116
        Employees........................116
        AS IS Disclaimer..................117
        Knowledge Qualifiers..............117
    Representations and Warranties Made
    by the Buyer..........................118
Pre-Closing Obligations..................119
Closing Date............................120
Employees..............................120
Taxes..................................120
Conditions Precedent....................120

Personal Liability for Entity Obligations...... 121
Non-Competition Restriction............. 122
Non-Solicitation Restriction.............. 123
Confidentiality; No Press Releases......... 124
Bulk Sales............................. 124
Indemnification 125
Brokers............................... 127
Boilerplate............................ 128
    Fees and Costs 128
    Severability...................... 129
    Entire Agreement or Merger 129
    Modification or Amendment 129
    Waiver.......................... 130
    Governing Law................... 130
    Venue 131
    Dispute Resolution 132
    Assignment or No Assignment 132
    Successors and Assigns 133
    Notices 134
    Headings 134
    Survival......................... 135
    Further Assurances 135
    Third-Party Beneficiaries........... 136
    Attorney's Fees Shifting............ 136
    Counterparts 137
    Independent Legal Counsel 138
Signature Block........................ 138
Paragraphs You Don't Need for a
Simultaneous Closing................... 139
Conclusion............................ 140

Chapter 12   What Happens Before Closing?............... 142
    Seller's Pre-Closing Work 142

    Operate in the Ordinary Course 142
    Maintain Inventory 143
    Help Obtain Consents 143
    Help with Employees 144
    Remove Excluded Assets. 145
    Bulk Sales Act Compliance. 146
   Buyer's Pre-Closing Work 146
    Set Up Acquisition Entity 146
    Conduct Due Diligence 147
    Obtain Financing 147
    Obtain Consents 148
    Obtain Licenses, Permits, or
    Government Permissions 149
    Obtain Insurance 149
    Line Up Employees. 149

Chapter 13 The Closing. 151
   Formal Versus Informal 151
   Closing Documents. 154
    Closing Checklist. 155
    Asset Purchase Agreement 155
    Side Agreements 155
    Bill of Sale 155
    Vehicle or Equipment Titles. 156
    Secretary's Certificate 156
    Bring-Down Certificate 157
    Assignment and Assumption of Lease . . . 157
    Assignment and Assumption of Other
    Contracts 157
    Assignment of Patents, Trademarks,
    Copyrights, and Other Intellectual
    Property Rights 158
    Settlement Statement 158

    Escrow Agreement 159
    Promissory Note 159
    Security Agreement 160
    Personal Guaranty 160
    Bank Loan Documents 160
   Keys, Passwords, Alarm Codes 161
   Purchase Price Payment and Disbursement .. 161
   Time Requirements 163

Chapter 14 What You Need to Do After Closing 164
    Training 164
    Transition of Customers, Vendors, and
    Suppliers 165
    Switching Over Utilities and Domain Name .. 165
    Recording Title Documents 166
    Recording Liens 167
    Obtaining Licenses, Permits, or other
    Government Approval 167
    Public Announcement 168
    Earn-Out 168

Chapter 15 The Deal is Done 170

Acknowledgments

Thanks to everyone who helped me get this idea out of my head and into a book.

Thanks to Jenny for listening to all my ideas and helping me realize the best ones. Her wisdom always helps me achieve my dreams. She also spent many hours editing my draft.

Thanks to Joshua, Caitlin, Jacob, Joseph, and Jess for creative input and reality checks.

Thanks to Von and Kari for setting the example and boosting my confidence.

Thanks to Murray for late afternoon head sessions on the beach at Emerald Isle, NC.

Thanks to Rick Minardi for trusting me with and mentoring me through my first deal.

Thanks to Taegan for letting me be her first author.

Thanks to Shay for the final edit.

Thanks to my clients for entrusting me with their deals.

About the Author

Joel Ankney is an elite Virginia attorney. By some reports, there are about one million lawyers in the United States, and many of them have probably helped clients buy a business. What makes Joel one in a million? It's his combination of academics, experience, and personality.

Joel graduated first in his class from William & Mary Law School, where he received several academic honors. He also holds a bachelor's degree in Psychology from Brigham Young University.

Joel has been practicing law for 25 years. Before opening his own law firm, he worked for large national and international law firms. Throughout his career, he has worked on deals that have ranged in purchase price from thousands to hundreds of millions of dollars. Joel's experience working on deals of all sizes has exposed him to the simplest and some of the most complex transactions. Since opening his law firm 13 years ago, Joel has closed more than $250 million in business deals. Joel typically works on deals with purchase prices ranging from $10,000 to $5 million.

Joel's experience in helping people buy or sell businesses comes from representing a variety of industries, such as:

- Software developers;
- Insurance agencies;
- Fitness clubs and yoga studios;
- Dental, orthodontics, physical therapy, chiropractic, veterinary, and physician practices;
- Restaurants;
- Online and brick-and-mortar retailers;
- Construction firms;
- Office equipment services;
- IT consultants;
- Hair salons;
- Franchises;
- Automotive service businesses; and
- Manufacturers.

As a result, Joel knows what questions to ask and what issues need to be addressed to protect his client's interests. Because of his experience, he can smoothly guide clients through the business-buying process because he knows what to look out for, what questions to ask, what to expect, what's customary, and what's reasonable.

When Joel isn't working with clients on deals, he can be found longboarding, paddling, or mountain biking. He enjoys sharing his love of fun and the outdoors with his four sons and wife, Jennifer. His family has lived and played in Virginia for over 29 years.

Preface

Chances are you have watched TV shows depicting trial lawyers. The media helps us form our perceptions of lawyers, but those perceptions (whether accurate or not) usually are limited to lawsuits and trials. Have you ever seen a TV show that depicts a business lawyer navigating a deal with a client?

A good business lawyer doesn't handle a deal the same way a good trial lawyer handles a trial. In fact, a business lawyer who approaches a business deal like a trial lawyer usually does more to harm the deal than help it.

A lawsuit is adversarial. The people involved disagree with each other. They want different outcomes—opposing outcomes. If one wins, the other loses; it's a fight. The trial lawyers are the hired guns, and their approach is usually very aggressive. They make demands and threats. They file motions. They argue about everything. If they are defending the case, they might engage in tactics that slow down the process. Their tactics might inflict pain on the other side. Then they use that pain as leverage to try to negotiate a settlement.

By contrast, a business purchase is a collaborative experience. The people involved want the same outcome—the sale and purchase of the business. They may have differing interests on certain terms of the deal, like purchase price, payment terms, or closing date, but they are usually willing to compromise to achieve the ultimate objective. The buyer and seller usually want the deal to progress at a reasonable pace, and threats and demands typically are counterproductive. The business lawyers should facilitate the deal, not create an environment that might kill the deal. They need to know which issues are important, which are not that significant, and how issues are customarily resolved—i.e., what's reasonable, rather than extreme. This is how Joel approaches deals.

This book teaches you how a deal works—the process. It will help you understand what to expect before, during, and after you close the deal. This book also explains the ins and outs of the key contract for the deal—the Asset Purchase Agreement.

I Am Not Your Lawyer Because You Read this Book

We need to take care of some business before we start. What I am about to write might sound a bit harsh, but it makes me sleep better. Lawyers call this a "Disclaimer."

Writing a book creates a risk for a lawyer, so I want to clear up our relationship from the beginning. A client can sue a lawyer for bad legal advice. Books by lawyers can create the impression that the reader is the author's client and that the author is giving the reader legal advice. This book is for informational purposes only. It is designed to help you understand the legal aspects of buying a business.

Although I am a lawyer, **I am not your lawyer**. Reading this book does not make me your lawyer and it doesn't make you my client. If you want me to become your lawyer, we can talk and, if we are both in agreement, go through the process of making that happen.

Also, I am licensed to practice law only in Virginia. The information in this book is based on my experiences practicing law in

Virginia. You might live in another state or country. The laws of your state or country might be different from Virginia's laws. If you want to know what the laws of your state or country are, you need to speak with a lawyer licensed in your state or country.

In addition, this book contains a number of stories to illustrate principles. All of the examples are based on true stories, although, in some instances, I have combined or slightly altered experiences and changed names in order to preserve client confidentiality or identity.

This book is not considered legal advice. It contains information about legal topics. You use the information in this book at your own risk.

If you want legal advice, you should hire a lawyer. I strongly encourage you to do so.

I'm available.

Law Office of Joel Ankney PC

www.jalawoffice.com

Introduction

Buying a small business is a process, not an event. Deciding to buy a business is just the first step. Once you have made that decision, you start a process that has many moving parts.

I am a business lawyer. I have been helping people buy businesses for over 20 years. I spend a great deal of time guiding my clients through the buying process. I educate them on what to expect, how long it will take, and what is customary and reasonable. I arm them with the information they need to make good decisions.

This book tells you what I know about buying a business. I wrote this book for three reasons: first, to teach you what your lawyer should know about buying a business; second, to help you avoid surprises; and third, to help you make better decisions during the buying process.

This book gives you a head start to buying a small business. Learn what your lawyer already knows, but may not tell you. Don't be left in the dark. This book will be a guide as you think about buying a business, or even if you are already in the middle of a deal.

The knowledge you gain from reading this book will have positive results. It can ease the stress you experience when buying a business, help you make better decisions during the buying process, improve your relationship with your lawyer (lawyer's love educated clients), and potentially decrease your legal fees (because your lawyer won't have to bill you for time spent educating you about the process).

CHAPTER 1

Evaluate Yourself First

Buying a small business is a life-changing experience. You should ask yourself two basic questions to determine if you are ready. First, should I own a business? And second, should I own <u>this</u> business? These questions focus on you, not the actual business opportunity.

I'm not trying to discourage anyone from buying a business, but I do want to provide a quick reality check. Answering these questions in the negative before you begin the business buying process will save you a lot of money, time, effort, and stress. On the other hand, answering them in the positive will fortify your commitment to the project.

Should I Own a Business?

Owning a business is not for everyone. You should evaluate your personality, skills, experience, and risk aversion to determine whether owning a business is the right move for you. There are a lot of other books, online assessments, and tools out there to help you evaluate whether you might have what it takes to be a successful business owner. This book is not designed to help you make that assessment, but that doesn't mean you should skip that step.

The one point I want to emphasize in this analysis is the risk. If you are risk averse, then owning your own business will be the most stressful thing you've ever done. Even if you have skills and experience, the reality of owning your own business means you will be taking on a lot of risks. One of the largest risks probably comes from taking on debt for money to buy and run the business. Some of the obligations associated with owning a business include: making payroll; paying taxes, vendors, and suppliers on time; paying the rent, and so on. Ideally, these obligations should come before your own interests. Meeting these obligations means you risk not getting paid if there isn't any money left over after paying the business's obligations. Can you live with that possibility? Can you live with the possibility of getting through lean times when the business doesn't have enough cash flow to pay its obligations? If you can't stomach that risk, then you should stop here.

I spent about 12 years working for large corporate law firms. It was demanding work that required being in the office for many hours, but I was compensated well with a regular paycheck and benefits. There was a lot of security associated with my job. When I contemplated opening my own law practice/business, I realized I would be giving up that security. I had several colleagues who had opened their own law practices. They were very gracious about sharing information about the nuts and bolts of opening and running a law practice. To help me determine whether I should own my own business, I read several books, researched online, but most importantly I asked those who had experienced what I was contemplating doing. I treated several friends and colleagues to lunches to "pick their brains" about the business side of a law practice. Some of them even gave me copies of their profit and loss statements to help me understand what I could expect in the way of revenues and expenses. This information helped me understand the reality of owning my own business. It was definitely a gut-check. I suggest you do the same type of research as you consider whether you want to own a business.

Should I Own **This** Business?

People often ask me whether I think they should buy a particular business. In order to help them, I always answer with questions, not about the deal, but about the individual. I'd like to share a few stories to help illustrate the importance of how questions about the individual as a prospective buyer can assist in evaluating whether to purchase a business or not.

<u>"Do You Love Dogs?"</u>
Like the Industry

Henry visited my office for a consultation about whether or not to buy a business. He had recently been downsized from a large company and was having difficulty finding a comparable job. He decided to take money from his severance package and retirement to purchase a dog grooming business he found through a business broker.

Henry came into my office and slid a draft of an Asset Purchase Agreement across the table to me and asked whether it looked like a good deal. Before even looking at the contract, I posed this question: "Do you love dogs?" My client was taken aback and looked puzzled. What did his perspective on dogs have to do with evaluating the proposed deal? I explained that if he didn't love dogs, then it didn't matter how good the deal was because he would hate owning the business, which would mean the business would most likely fail.

Can You Weather the Storm?
Understand the Business Model

Jane left employment in midlife with a large, international corporation. She used her severance package to purchase a franchise that sold furniture. She had never been a part of the furniture industry and wasn't familiar with how furniture stores operate. She purchased the franchise and almost immediately had several disagreements with the franchisor, believing she had found better solutions to operational issues than the franchisor provided.

The business model consisted of a retail store with floor models of the furniture. There was little to no inventory in the store. A customer would select furniture and place an order. The store would take a small percentage of the purchase price as a down payment, and then order the furniture for delivery within about four to six weeks. What my client didn't realize before she bought the business was that she would have to pay the full wholesale price to the supplier prior to getting the furniture. In other words, she would have to advance her business's money to pay for the furniture at least four to six weeks (or more) before she would collect the customer's balance of the retail price. This created a significant, unforeseen, negative impact on her cash flow.

Already in a bad cash flow position, disaster occurred - literally. A large water pipe burst in the neighboring store on a weekend and flooded the furniture store. She had insurance but didn't have the cash flow to keep the store open until the insurance claim was paid. She had no other choice but to close down the business.

In my opinion, not understanding the cash flow reality of the furniture business was the first domino. Once it tipped over, the rest of the dominoes leading to the business closing fell quickly.

How Do You Feel About Working the Line?
Experience in the Industry

Gary had been a Chief Financial Officer at a manufacturing company. He was downsized, had been out of work for some time, and, as a result, was discouraged by his job search. He had some money saved up and found a Subway franchise for sale in a neighboring town. He sought me out and asked for input on whether I thought buying the franchise was a good idea for him.

Some of the first questions I asked were whether he had ever worked in the restaurant industry? Did he know about fast-food restaurant operations? Had he ever managed teenagers or low wage employees? Was he prepared to work on the restaurant line making sandwiches and prepping food when an employee didn't show up? He replied in the negative to these questions and told me that those things would never happen. In my experience, however, I knew there was a high probability they would.

At the end of our meeting, I suggested a restaurant might not be a good fit for him, that he already was fighting an uphill battle because of his lack of experience and knowledge.

These stories illustrate three principles that I try to teach people about owning a business.

First, you need to <u>like the industry</u>—even have a passion for it. Don't buy a dog grooming business if you don't have a passion for dogs.

Second, you need to <u>understand the business model</u>—the way the business works. This will help you assess the potential risks associated with the business. You need to understand cash flow, revenues, expenses, seasons, business cycles, etc. Understanding the business model will help you determine whether you can weather future storms, because they will come.

Third, you need to determine your <u>experience in the industry</u>. For example, being in the restaurant business is tough; it usually requires a significant human investment by the owner. Most restaurant owners I have worked with basically live at the restaurant. They are working there even when the restaurant is closed (e.g., preparing food for the next day, managing workers, ordering food, paying bills, etc.). You will avoid a lot of surprises and frustration if you already have experience in the industry.

I don't like to see people start a project at a disadvantage. When someone asks me whether I think a business is right for him, they want me to evaluate the business opportunity, not the individual business owner, but, in my opinion, self-evaluation is the first step to buying a small business, and can screen out significant risks disguised as opportunities.

Once you have evaluated yourself and determined you want to move forward, then it's time to assemble your team.

CHAPTER 2

ASSEMBLE YOUR TEAM

I like to say that life is a team sport. You increase your chances of success if others help you. Even professional athletes who play individual sports like golf have a team behind them (e.g., caddie, swing coach, spouse, agent, sponsors). Like an athlete, you'll want a team of advisers and experts to help you evaluate the small business you want to purchase and to help guide you through the buying process. If you try to go it alone, you significantly increase your risk of failure.

Assemble Your Team at the Beginning of the Deal

Many business buyers believe they can save on fees if they wait until the last minute to involve advisers. If you try to pick up team members as the deal progresses, you put them at a disadvantage, which will hurt your deal. For example, your accountant's evaluation of the purchase price is of no real help to you if you ask for her input after you have agreed in principle to the price. Likewise, if you wait until just before the closing to have a business lawyer review the Purchase Agreement, his input will have less of an impact because you won't be able to go back and renegotiate issues he identifies.

Who Should Be On Your Team?
At a minimum, I recommend you involve your close confidant, a business lawyer, and an accountant. You might also consider using a business broker. If you are financing your purchase with a loan, you will want some involvement from the loan officer.

Close Confidant
A close confidant should be your first team member. A close confidant is a person you trust with private matters, someone whose opinion you value. Usually this is your spouse or significant other. Your confidant should be involved from the very beginning when you first start toying with the idea of buying a business. She doesn't need business expertise to contribute to the deal. This person will be a sounding board for your ideas. Her questions, reactions, and advice will help you better evaluate your plans.

Buying a business is risky. Your confidant will be taking that risk with you. That's reason enough to involve her. But you also may find she sees things from a different perspective that can add to your evaluation of the business deal. She might have some questions or insight you never considered.

When you first propose the idea of buying a business, your confidant's initial reaction might be negative or critical. That's natural for most people because you are suggesting a life-changing event that will impact her security—financial, lifestyle, and relationship. Her negative or critical reaction might be a type of defense mechanism to preserve that security.

You might also become defensive if your confidant initially challenges your decision to buy a business. Fight that urge. You want to involve your confidant to gain her valuable counsel and support. That won't happen if your discussion escalates into an argument. I suggest you plan out what you want to say to your confidant, rather than winging it. You will have a better chance persuading her to take the risk with you if you are able to clearly explain your thoughts and analysis that have lead you to your preliminary decision. You also increase your chances of gaining support if you can help your confidant understand and quantify the potential risks and how you plan to reduce them.

There is no limit to the amount of time you will need to counsel with your confidant. Have multiple conversations. You may need some cooling off periods. If you feel pressured by an artificial deadline to move forward without your confidant because you believe you will lose the opportunity to buy the business you are considering, step back and work toward gaining your confidant's support, rather than jumping on a deal. Other deals will always come along.

When your close confidant joins your team and supports your decision, she will become your strongest ally and supporter. When I shared my idea about starting my own law practice with my wife and my plan for doing so in a way that would decrease some of the risks, her support and help with meeting financial goals and launching the practice was invaluable. She became my coach, cheerleader, accountability partner, and manager. She was the driving force in helping me turn my idea into reality. The same can happen for you. You will find that a supportive close confidant is your most valuable team member.

Business Lawyer
When negotiating and closing a deal, having a business lawyer on your team is invaluable. When you buy a small business, you will sign a contract. The contract will require you to pay a large sum of money for the business and will allocate risks between the seller and the buyer. Why would you negotiate and sign such an important contract without having a lawyer help you?

John brought his son into see me for a consultation. His son was buying a retail business and John thought that using a business lawyer would help his son avoid some risks. His son was not interested in retaining a business lawyer, even after I explained how I could help. The son was the manager of the business and trusted the owner. The son did not retain me. About six months later, the son called me. He had closed the deal without a business lawyer. After closing, he discovered that the seller was in default of the lease, the seller did not get the landlord's consent to the sale, and the seller had liens against the assets for unpaid taxes. He was in jeopardy of losing the business and all the money he paid for it. Had he used a business lawyer, these problems would have been identified and resolved before closing.

Engage a seasoned business lawyer at the beginning of your deal. Doing so saves time, frustration, and legal fees. There are lots of lawyers out there focusing on their chosen specialty, most of which would be happy to represent you, but you should make sure you hire a business lawyer, not a trial lawyer—there is a difference. Trial lawyers are good for lawsuits, but their adversarial approach to resolving disputes usually harms a business deal. In addition, their lack of regular experiences with negotiating and closing business deals usually means they are not good at spotting risks and issues involved in deals. They won't be able to filter or prioritize issues because they don't understand what is customary and reasonable. If I learn that a trial attorney is involved in a deal, red flags go up, and I anticipate a difficult negotiation, poorly drafted documents that will require lots of re-drafting, and unproductive gamesmanship and tactics. Because of these tactics, your legal fees also will increase due to drawn out and unnecessary negotiations.

Having a seasoned business lawyer on your team will be one of your best assets.

Your business lawyer can see that the contract and other deal documents are enforceable. For example, under Virginia law an agreement to agree is unenforceable. Clients frequently come to me with contracts that contain provisions indicating that the buyer and seller will decide on some key term after closing, such as purchase price, payment terms, or post-closing compensation for the seller. Such a provision probably is not enforceable. As a result, without a business lawyer's help, some of the most important parts of the deal would be invalid. Without a business lawyer's help, the buyer probably would not even realize this fatal mistake until sometime after closing. Regrettably, at that time it's too late to fix the problem. As a direct result, the buyer has potentially purchased a lawsuit against the seller, rather than a business. That's not a great start to a successful business.

Your business lawyer also can advise you on what is customary and reasonable for a deal. That advice comes from the experience of handling many deals and from knowing what is locally acceptable. Deals in California and New York look different than deals in Virginia because not only are the laws different, but there also are differences in what are acceptable, customary, and reasonable practices in the local business community. Without a seasoned business lawyer, you might enter into a contract with unreasonable terms without realizing it. Again, you probably would not discover this mistake until you had a disagreement with the seller after closing.

Related to knowing what is customary and reasonable is your business lawyer's ability to spot issues when something is missing. The Purchase Agreement may be silent on key issues. Without a seasoned business lawyer, you probably would not even know that language is missing. Signing a contract that fails to address key issues will create big problems for you after closing, such as putting on you the responsibility to pay for things you should not customarily pay for or assuming liabilities and responsibilities that you customarily should not assume.

Another benefit of having a business lawyer who knows what is customary and reasonable relates to how negotiations will proceed. Your business lawyer should be able to filter and prioritize the issues to be negotiated based on that knowledge. It makes no sense to fight over issues and deal points that you likely won't get. Focusing on unreasonable or uncustomary issues will also destroy your credibility, which will significantly impact your strength and position for the rest of the deal process. You will get much better results by using a business lawyer to help you filter and prioritize issues.

The benefit of having a seasoned business lawyer who knows what is customary and reasonable significantly contributes to your risk management. One of the main purposes of the Purchase Agreement is to allocate risks associated with the business between the seller and the buyer. Without a business lawyer, you probably will take on risks the seller should retain.

A side note about lawsuits:

- You'll want to avoid them because they are time-consuming, expensive, and emotionally draining;
- They will take your focus off your business;
- You will end up paying lawyers lots of fees;
- You will suffer significant stress;
- The lawsuit will take a considerable amount of time to resolve;
- You will be the target of massive document production requests and depositions;
- The outcome always is uncertain; and
- Even if you "win," you will have expended significant amounts of money, time, and emotional energy, which could have otherwise been put into your business.

Engaging a seasoned business lawyer reduces the risk of a lawsuit through expert contract drafting and negotiation.

A seasoned business lawyer can guide and help you through the process of buying the business. Buying a business is not like buying a car. You don't just sign a contract, pay the purchase price, and walk out with the keys. Buying a business is more like buying a house, where you look at the house before signing the contract, sign the contract, obtain your financing, conduct home and pest inspections, close the purchase, and then deal with post-closing issues. But even the home-buying analogy falls short because buying a business has several more steps and documents than buying a house. You want a seasoned business lawyer on your team as your guide through the entire process.

Frankly, buying a business without a seasoned business lawyer on your team is like jumping out of an airplane without a parachute.

Accountant
An accountant will help decipher and analyze the financial data of the business you want to buy. An accountant's input will significantly help you evaluate the business deal, and as a result may help you avoid a bad deal.

<u>The Overpriced Dental Practice</u>

Bethany engaged me to help her purchase a dental practice. She had recently stepped in temporarily to take care of the practice's patients after the original owner had passed away. Now the original owner's widow was offering to sell her the practice.

Bethany shared with me the proposed Purchase Agreement and financial information. My initial reaction was that the purchase price seemed unreasonably high, but my background is not in financial analysis. I learned that Bethany already had an accountant on her team of advisers. I suggested we ask the accountant to review the financial data and give us his initial impression about the purchase price.

The accountant only needed a short time to confirm that the purchase price was unreasonably high.

The widow valued her late husband's reputation in the community and patient list to be much greater than was reasonable. The accountant pointed out that it would be virtually impossible for Bethany to service the debt she would take on to finance the purchase price with the revenues the practice generated. Armed with that information, Bethany attempted to negotiate a lower purchase price. When the widow refused to negotiate the purchase price, Bethany walked away from the deal.

We learned later that another dentist purchased the practice for the same price the widow asked Bethany to pay. The seller shared with the buyer about Bethany and her decision not to buy the practice. About three months after the buyer purchased the practice, he called Bethany to ask why she did not buy the practice. The new dentist explained that after only three months, he was unable to make the payments on the loan he took out to finance the purchase because the practice was not generating enough revenues.

From this one example, you can probably understand how important an accountant's input is to a prospective buyer. Bethany had dodged a bullet that would have financially ruined her. Bethany's story does have a happy ending because she was able to find another practice to purchase on much more reasonable terms.

You also will need an accountant after you buy the business to help you set up and transition your payroll, bookkeeping, and financial systems and advise you on tax planning strategies. You will need him to help you prepare financial statements (e.g., for your lender) and your state and federal tax returns. Your accountant's input will benefit you before and for many years after you buy the business.

Business Broker
Buyers usually do not engage brokers to represent them, but they sometimes contact brokers to see the list of businesses the brokers are offering for sale. A broker usually will not be a member of your team but can help you find a business to buy.

A business broker helps sellers find buyers for their businesses. The business broker maintains a list of sellers who have agreed to list their businesses exclusively with that particular broker. The business broker's primary purposes are to find buyers, establish and shepherd the relationship between the seller and the prospective buyer, and to help the parties negotiate the essential terms of the deal.

The broker customarily represents the seller and protects her best interests. In addition, a broker gets paid a commission for closing the deal. The commission usually is a percentage of the purchase price (e.g., 10%). The seller pays the broker's commission out of the proceeds she receives from the sale. As a result, you should understand that the broker's loyalty is to the seller, not you. The commission also acts as a significant incentive for the broker to get you to close the deal. If the deal does not close, the broker does not get paid. Can you see how these factors might result in a broker pushing you to give in on certain issues during negotiations so the deal will close?

Many brokers also offer form deal documents, like letters of intent and Purchase Agreements, to use when buying a business. My observation is that they do this because they believe the deal already is in hand and the documents are merely a formality. Remember that these documents provided by the broker are legally binding documents that typically are not drafted by or negotiated with the help of an attorney. They usually are brief and leave out a lot of important points. They also take a "one-size-fits-all" approach, meaning that they do not address issues that are relevant to certain industries or deals. Several of these form documents have crossed my desk. They have been horribly drafted and do not represent the buyer's interests. Many times I do not get to see them until after the buyer has signed them, which usually means I have been brought in too late in the game to do anything other than emergency damage control. A broker is not a lawyer. Always be very cautious about using legal documents provided by the broker.

Many brokers also do not like a buyer to involve a business lawyer in the deal. They feel that the lawyer will slow down the process and raise issues that might jeopardize the deal. The broker fears her commission might be at risk if the lawyer bogs down or even kills the deal by her involvement. As a buyer, you should not care about the broker's concerns. Instead, you should care about having a lawyer on your team who will represent and protect your best interests. If you involve a good business lawyer on your team, then she will be working to make the deal happen, not kill it.

If you involve a business broker in your deal, use them for their strengths, i.e., finding a deal, relationship building, and essential term negotiation, and realize that they do not represent your best interests because they represent the seller. Also, do not let the broker take the place of a lawyer or discourage you from engaging a lawyer.

Banker or Loan Officer

You will need a lender if you need to borrow money to finance the purchase. The lender will designate a representative to negotiate your loan and be your point of contact. This banker or loan officer can provide input on what is customary and reasonable for a deal.

How to Find Team Members

Finding people who know how to do a business deal well and whom you can trust to protect your best interests takes work. Nowadays, it's common for people to search for help using the Internet. The Internet can provide useful information about potential team members, but it probably isn't the best place to start.

The best way to identify potential advisers for your team is to ask other people. Ask the people you trust whom they trust. Asking friends and family is a good start, but they may not have needed an adviser for a business deal. Consider asking other business owners and other professionals whom they would recommend.

Don't try to identify all of your advisers at the same time. You should start by looking for one adviser—a business lawyer, accountant, or lender. Once you have identified that first adviser, then ask them to suggest other advisers. Most business lawyers, accountants, and loan officers usually have a group of other advisers they trust. Often these people work together efficiently because they have similar personalities and approaches to getting deals done. If you were to engage me as your business attorney, I would willingly recommend an accountant and loan officer with whom I have had positive experiences working on deals. They are professional and take care of my clients, so I always want them involved. Because my clients have given me frequent positive feedback about the accountant and loan officer, I know my recommendations are sound. In addition, they approach working on business deals the same way I do (e.g., they work cooperatively to make deals, rather than combatively in a manner that might break the deal).

Receiving recommendations should not be the end of your vetting process, however. You should research the recommendations. This is where the Internet can help. Check out the website for each recommended individual. Do they clearly have business deal experience? Do they focus on business deals, or does their business deal practice seem like a small portion of their practice? Are they too big or too small for you? For example, you probably don't want to engage a business lawyer at a large law firm to purchase a small business because the legal fees will be disproportionally large.

Interview your potential advisers. Even if they look good on paper (or on their website), I recommend you meet each adviser for about 30 minutes to determine whether the information you heard and read about them rings true (some professionals are great at puffing on their websites). Tell them when you make the appointment that you are interviewing advisers to help with an upcoming purchase of a business. They usually are willing to meet with you for a period of time, at no cost, as a marketing effort to attract a potential client.

When you meet with potential advisers, you should determine whether their personality and approach to doing deals fits well with yours. Can you work with this person? Buying a business is stressful enough, so you don't want to multiply that stress by engaging an adviser with whom you don't get along well. Limit your questions to making those determinations. Don't try to get free advice from them. They won't appreciate that tactic and might be less inclined to want to work with you if they feel like you are taking advantage of them.

Some potential clients like to imply or suggest that if they are inclined to engage an adviser, they might use them for other projects after the deal has closed. I suggest you not bring up that possibility during your interview. Many seasoned professionals understand that when they do a good job on a business purchase, you probably will engage them for future projects. If you dangle that possibility in front of them during the interview, however, the professional might sense you are trying to manipulate him, and that's not a good way to start a relationship.

Get Your Team in Place Early
Once you have decided to buy a business, your next big step should be to assemble your team of advisers. This is a significant business decision that will impact your experience for good or bad during the deal process. Good advisers will help you avoid or smoothly resolve problems. The earlier in the process you select your team, the better prepared you will be when issues and challenges arise during the deal.

CHAPTER 3

Finding Your Target

Lawyers call the business you decide to buy the "target." Before you start looking, you should determine your criteria for your ideal target. Your approach in developing your criteria should be similar to the approach you would take when developing a wish list for a home you want to buy, such as purchase price range, location, cash flow range, type of business, and the industry you desire. Write that criteria down as part of your acquisition plan. You wouldn't buy a home without first creating a list of what you want. Likewise, you shouldn't buy a business without a similar list.

There are a lot of small businesses for sale. My clients have found their targets many different ways. There is no one way or correct way to find your target. Following are some suggestions for finding your target.

Employee Purchase

Some clients have found their target by asking their employer if they can purchase the business. This is very common in a healthcare setting, where a physician, dentist, or veterinarian frequently hires a younger professional as an employee with the intent and mutual understanding that the employee will have the option to buy part or all of the practice in the future.

Financially Struggling Businesses

Flora, an entrepreneur, buys small, independently owned pizza restaurants that are struggling financially. Because they are struggling, she usually purchases them for a reasonable price. She then works in the business herself to turn it around. One of the first things she does is hire new employees, including a restaurant manager, who can not only help turn around the restaurant but also might be a candidate to purchase the business in the near future. When the restaurant becomes more successful, the entrepreneur offers to sell it to the manager.

Owner Aging Out

The pattern above also extends to businesses owned by aging individuals who have no heir apparent to the business. An aging small business owner usually prefers to sell the business to get paid for the sweat equity invested in the business. The only way to cash in on that sweat equity is to sell. If the business owner simply shuts down and walks away from the business, he has lost the invested sweat equity. As a result, an aging small business owner is usually very open to selling the business. Usually, the most likely candidate is a trusted employee. If you are employed by an aging business owner, and you consider yourself a trusted employee, and you want to stay in that business, approach the business owner and express your desire to explore purchasing the business when the owner is ready to retire or exit.

Competitors

Some people find their target by looking at competitors. Roxanne owned a specialty retail clothing store. She regularly ate lunch and kept in touch with one of her competitors. The competitor politely made it known on several occasions that she would be interested in buying Roxanne's business if she ever decided to sell. The timing was right when she mentioned this one day, and Roxanne offered up her business for sale.

Customers

Other people find their target by asking the owner of one of their favorite businesses if they would be willing to sell. At one time, I represented a local bar that was sold to one of their regular customers. The customer had always wanted to own a bar and made his intent known to the owner on a number of occasions. The owner reached a point where he wanted to exit the business and offered up the bar to the customer. The customer's patience and persistence paid off.

One woman frequented a gift shop near her local beach. When she expressed her interest to the owner about how great it would be to own a shop at the beach, she discovered that the owner was looking to retire. The shop owner offered to sell the gift shop to the woman.

Word of Mouth

Some people find their target business by asking around. They ask friends and family members if they know of anyone who might have a business to sell. I have observed that if you tell a lot of people you are interested in buying a business, someone will know of an opportunity.

Listings

Other people find their target business by researching listings of businesses for sale. These listings appear in newspaper classified ads and online. A simple Google search will identify several websites that list local businesses for sale. Some of those websites are maintained by business brokers. Craigslist also has a category where you can find businesses for sale. The credibility of Internet listings may be suspect, however. As with all offers on the Internet, you need to be highly vigilant to protect against scams. Do not give out your private personal information no matter how good the deal looks in the listing.

Brokers

I also have worked with many people who have discovered their target by contacting local business brokers. Brokers keep a list of businesses for sale, similar to the listings of homes for sale kept by realtors. You should understand that a broker's list is limited to only those sellers the broker represents. Therefore, if you decide to pursue this method, you should consider contacting multiple brokers. Remember, the broker will not be representing you, so you do not need to feel any loyalty to the broker. As a buyer, you are under no obligation to work exclusively with any one broker.

Franchises

Finally, if you are looking to purchase a franchise, you can contact a franchisor directly. If the franchisor doesn't have a franchisee in your area, you might be able to buy the franchise directly from the franchisor. Many franchisors will also know of franchisees in your area who are looking to sell. Franchise listings also exist online. Some listings are for existing franchisees attempting to sell their franchises; other listings are for franchisors selling franchise opportunities.

The reality is that many businesses are for sale. Lots of sources exist for finding your target. You won't have difficulty finding businesses for sale, but be selective. Explore those sources to determine which seem to be the most effective for finding a target business that fits your criteria. This approach will increase your chances for success.

CHAPTER 4

VALUING THE TARGET BUSINESS

One of the first deal terms you will negotiate is the purchase price. Once you have found a business to buy, how do you determine whether it is overpriced, underpriced, or reasonably priced? You need to collect as much information as possible in a short period of time to help reduce your stress about the risks of buying the target business.

You can reduce your stress associated with buying a business when you determine that you are paying a reasonable price for the business. This chapter walks you through different tools that may assist you in the valuation process.

To start with, the seller sets the purchase price for the business. She may have done this in several different ways:

- She may have determined the price with input from her accountant and broker;
- She may have set the price based on her analysis of the business's financials;
- She may have set the price using some conventional methodology or rule of thumb, such as a multiple of discretionary earnings;

- She may have hired a valuation expert or appraiser to value the business (this is rare for small businesses);
- She may have just pulled a number out of the air based on what she feels the business is worth; or
- She may have used a combination of these approaches.

Ask the seller to explain her approach for determining the purchase price. Her response will not only help you determine the reasonableness of the price but also might identify opportunities for negotiating the price. If the seller engaged a valuation expert or appraiser, you can ask for a copy of the report or appraisal. Be aware that the seller is under no obligation to share the report with you and might be reluctant to do so if it points out weaknesses with the business.

Do your own research. If a broker is involved, you can ask him to provide some examples of other similar businesses for sale to compare the purchase prices. If there is no broker or if the broker is unwilling to provide that information, you can do your own research on the Internet to find listings of comparable businesses for sale.

Because you already have an accountant on your team, at the very least, have your accountant review the target business's financials and tax returns. Have him look at the past three to five years' worth of information. Your accountant will be able to see trends, analyze cash flow, and flag anomalies that might indicate deeper problems with the business. He can help you understand the potential for the business to service the debt you might take on to pay the purchase price.

Hiring your own valuation expert or appraiser may benefit you because he will look at comparable businesses for sale, analyze financial information, and apply rules of thumb using his experience. A valuation report or appraisal will usually provide you with very reliable information to help evaluate the purchase price. It also may provide ammunition for negotiating a lower purchase price. Buyers typically do not engage a valuation expert or an appraiser, however, because of the expense. Fees can start at approximately $3,000 and go up from there depending on the size of the target business and complexity and detail of the review.

There are online valuation services where you can enter all of the financial data you have and get a valuation report. Those services cost around $400 to $500, but because I have no experience with them, I cannot speak to their accuracy or credibility. While using such a service won't hurt (other than the fee), it's unclear how much benefit you can gain from it. Instead, I suggest spending that fee on your accountant for his input on the purchase price.

If you are getting a loan for all or part of the purchase price, then your lender probably will require an appraisal of the target business. The lender will retain an approved appraiser to conduct the appraisal and require you to pay the appraisal fee as part of the lender's closing costs. That appraisal will come too late in the game for you, however. You usually will already have signed the Purchase Agreement with the agreed upon purchase price before your lender will order the appraisal. Hopefully, your business lawyer has seen that the Purchase Agreement contains a contingency that allows you to get out of the deal if you cannot obtain reasonable financing. In that case, if the lender's appraisal comes in lower than the purchase price, you will have the right to terminate the deal. Exercising that right might motivate the seller to renegotiate the price, or the seller may simply allow you to walk away so that she can look for another buyer willing to pay her asking price.

You may also be tempted to ask for your business lawyer's input on the reasonableness of the purchase price. Frankly, most business lawyers, even the most experienced, probably don't have the skills to evaluate the purchase price, unless they have some additional training or education. You are engaging them for their legal expertise, not financial services. Business lawyers typically will defer to the other experts on your team to evaluate the price.

Don't rely solely on the seller's purchase price determination. If you feel the price is too high, use your team members to help you evaluate its reasonableness and to develop logical bases for making a counteroffer. Completing a purchase price evaluation will help you avoid the risk of paying too much. On the other hand, determining that the purchase price is reasonable will solidify your resolve to purchase the business.

CHAPTER 5

Prepare for Hidden Costs

The purchase price is not the only cost associated with buying a new business. One of the worst experiences a lawyer can have is sharing a settlement statement with his client a few days before the closing that includes additional costs and expenses the buyer didn't anticipate.

This chapter helps you understand and anticipate the additional costs and expenses you will pay before or at closing. Understanding these costs and expenses at the beginning of the business buying process also might help you when evaluating which business to buy. For example, if you are looking for a business in the price range of $100,000 to $150,000, and understand that you might incur an additional $10,000 in costs and expenses associated with buying the business, you should adjust your target purchase price range to compensate for those additional costs (e.g., shifting your purchase price range down to $90,000 to $140,000).

In many instances, you will need to bring a check to closing to pay for the additional closing costs. It's important to understand these costs in order to be financially prepared to pay for them at closing.

Additional closing costs can include everything from costs associated with inspections, professional fees, utilities, and taxes, to the expenses of obtaining financing and approvals for transferring contracts. Below, I describe some of the more common categories of closing costs, although this list is not necessarily exhaustive. As you put your deal together, I suggest you discover your closing costs as soon as possible and keep a running, written tally of their estimated amounts.

Lender Financing Costs

Your lender will charge you fees and costs associated with obtaining the loan to finance the purchase price. The lender may require you to pay the following fees:

- Loan commitment fee, usually determined by the size of the loan;
- Lender-required appraisal;
- The lender's attorney's fees; and
- The recording costs of any liens against the business to protect the lender's collateral.

A lender will have you pay some of the fees up front and the rest at closing. For example, you usually are required to pay the loan commitment fee when you sign the loan commitment letter. That fee might be several thousand dollars. Some lenders also might require that you pay for the appraisal up front, and others will let you pay for it at closing.

Some lenders will allow you to fold some of the closing costs into the loan as part of a promotional lending program or offer. In other words, they will increase the loan amount by enough money to cover many of the closing costs, essentially allowing you to borrow the closing costs. If you don't have the money for the closing costs, you should ask your lender about this possibility.

Other lenders may have special programs or limited-time offers for which they will agree to pay some or all of the closing costs without including them in the amount of the loan. Again, you should ask your lender if that possibility exists.

Raising Capital

You might decide to bring investors into your deal to raise some or all of the money you need to buy the target business and operate it in the near-term after closing. I describe this process in more detail in Chapter 6, along with the costs and expenses associated with that process. If you plan on bringing in investors to raise capital, you should include the costs and expenses of that process in your calculation of the total fees and costs for the business deal.

Professional Fees

You need professional help when buying a business. At the least, I recommend you engage an accountant and a business lawyer. These professionals usually calculate their fees based on the amount of time they spend working on the project. They usually have an hourly rate, which they multiply by the number of hours (or partial hours) they spend working on the project. Some professionals might charge a flat rate for working on a deal, but that is not as common.

During your initial interview, ask your professional advisers how they will calculate their fees, what their estimated fees might be, and how they expect to be paid. Most professionals who have worked on many business deals should be able to give you a ballpark estimate of what their fees will be in connection with your deal. It's probably a red flag if a professional cannot estimate his fees because that might indicate a lack of experience with business deals.

Professional fees will vary by geographic market. In Virginia, where I practice, hourly rates for business lawyers range from $250 to $600. If you are in a larger market, such as New York City or San Francisco, expect that range to be much higher. The amount of professional services required to negotiate and close your deal will be a function of its size and complexity. For example, you should incur lower fees for a deal to buy a one-office construction company for which you will pay cash and higher fees for a deal to buy a multi-location restaurant, for which you are borrowing most of the money from a bank to pay the purchase price. The more you can tell your lawyer and accountant up front about the deal, the better estimate you should be able to get from them.

It is impossible to tell the amount of legal fees to expect for a particular deal because each deal is unique. At the time I am writing this book, I can tell you that based on my experience in my geographic market, my clients can expect to pay approximately $5,000 to $7,500 in legal fees for deals that range in purchase price from $250,000 to $5,000,000 which are financed by a loan. I can also tell you that a lower purchase price does not necessarily result in lower legal fees because the legal work associated with negotiating and closing a business purchase and an associated loan generally are the same, even if the purchase price is lower than $250,000. For smaller deals, however, I suggest considering spending at least $2,500 to $3,000 on legal fees, especially if you are paying cash for the business.

Accountants' fees also will vary by geographic market. For example, where I practice, hourly rates for accountants range from $175 to $375. Once again, those rates will be higher in larger markets. Your accountant probably will not be as heavily involved in the deal process as your business lawyer, so you should expect your accountant's fees to be less than your business lawyer's fees.

Retainers
Professionals also have varying approaches to getting paid their fees for working on the deal. Some may require an advance of part of the estimated fees when you engage them. For example, if a business lawyer estimates that her fees will be $5,000 to negotiate and close the deal, she may ask for $2,500 up front and the balance at some future time (more on that below). The attorney should deposit your advance into her attorney trust account and only draw money out as services are performed and fees are incurred and invoiced.

Pay-As-You-Go
Other professionals may require that you pay on a monthly basis as fees are incurred and invoiced. This is the pay-as-you-go approach. A professional might require these payment terms if the deal process will take a long time to avoid performing a significant amount of services without getting paid for many months.

Defer to Closing
Still other professionals might be willing to defer their fees until the closing. The total amount of their fees would then be added as additional closing costs to the settlement statement, and you would be required to pay all of their fees

at the closing. This is an attractive approach if you will be borrowing money to pay your professional fees because you will obtain the loan proceeds at closing.

Negotiate
Professional fees and payment terms usually are negotiable. For example, if a lawyer requires an advance, you probably can negotiate the amount of the advance (e.g., 40%, instead of 50%). You might also be able to negotiate a cap on the total amount of fees (e.g., the lawyer will bill by the hour, but will not bill more than $7,500 in total for her services). In addition, you probably can negotiate when you will pay, especially if you have a reasonable basis for asking for certain payment terms. For example, if your loan amount will include funding for closing costs, you probably can negotiate to pay some or all of your professional fees at closing. A professional might be willing to defer her fees until closing if she has an assurance that you will have the money then (as part of the loan proceeds) and the closing is not too far away.

Note, however, that you will be required to pay your professional fees regardless of whether you close the deal or not.

Inspection Costs
Consider engaging certain inspectors to help you evaluate the condition of the business or its assets before you close the deal.

Valuation Expert
If you engage a valuation expert to evaluate the purchase price for the business, you will be required to pay his fee.

The valuation expert will usually require payment of the fee when he delivers his valuation report. Some valuation experts may require payment of part of the fee when you engage them, with the balance due upon delivery of the report. The valuation expert probably will not agree to defer payment of his fee until closing.

Environmental Assessment
Liability for environmental problems can be a huge risk when buying a business. If you are concerned about the environmental condition of the property on which the business is located, then you should consider retaining an environmental engineering firm to perform a Phase I Environmental Assessment. For example, if you are buying a convenience store that sells gasoline, you should seriously consider inspecting the property for environmental issues, even if you will be leasing the property. If the target business customarily has environmental risks, a lender also may require a Phase I Environmental Assessment as a condition to loaning the purchase price money.

The environmental engineer will research past uses of the property and records about past environmental incidents at the property (e.g., spills and reported remediation efforts). She also will visit the property for a visual inspection and to interview personnel about their knowledge of any environmental issues at or near the property. The engineer will prepare and deliver to you a report that identifies any potential environmental problems and risks.

The Phase I Environmental Assessment can cost several thousands of dollars. You likely will need to pay the environmental engineer firm before closing. A common practice in my area is to pay one-half of the fee when you engage the engineer and the other half when the engineer finishes her work.

HVAC and Renovation Inspections

If you are leasing space for your new business, the lease might require you to be responsible for certain features at the leased space. For example, in Virginia, it is not uncommon for a landlord to require that the tenant be responsible for maintaining, repairing, and replacing the heating, air conditioning, and ventilation (HVAC) system. As a result, you should seriously consider engaging an HVAC contractor to inspect the HVAC system before you buy the business and sign the lease. The HVAC contractor should be able to tell you the condition of the HVAC system, any immediate repairs that might be needed, and a general idea of when the HVAC system might need to be replaced. This inspection might cost you a few hundred dollars. The HVAC contractor will require payment as soon as the inspection is complete.

Another additional cost associated with leasing property is the cost of renovating or building out the space. This cost typically is not incurred before or at closing; it usually is paid shortly after closing. Nevertheless, you should get estimates for that work as soon as possible before closing in order to factor that additional cost into the costs of buying the business. Having those estimates will also help you determine how much money you need to borrow to cover the purchase price and the post-closing renovations or build-out.

Equipment and Machinery Inspections

Finally, if you are buying equipment or machinery as part of the new business, you should consider having those assets inspected to determine whether they are in good working order.

Prorated Expenses & Taxes

The target business incurs certain operating expenses, such as utilities (electricity, gas, water, and sewer), rent, waste disposal, janitorial expenses, and personal property taxes. Many of those expenses are paid in advance monthly. As a result, if the seller pays those expenses before closing, you will be required to reimburse the seller for a pro rata portion of those expenses at closing. For example, if rent is $1,500 per month, the seller pays the rent on the first of the month, and the closing occurs on the 15th of the month, then you will be required to reimburse the seller for $750 of rent to pay for the portion of the month that occurs after closing. The same prorations will be calculated for other operating expenses the seller pays for prior to closing. You will need to bring that extra money to closing to reimburse the seller for those prorated expenses.

Security Deposit

If the target business leases space, it probably paid a security deposit to its landlord. The security deposit usually equals one month's rent. The seller is entitled to a refund of its security deposit when it terminates or transfers the lease unless it has damaged the leased space. You will need to pay the security deposit when you sign a new lease or acquire the seller's lease.

Depending on how you work things out with the landlord and the seller, you may have two different ways to pay the security deposit. First, you can pay a new security deposit to the landlord; then the landlord will refund the original security deposit to the seller. Second, and more customary, the landlord and seller may agree to transfer the original security deposit to you at closing. In that event, you will then reimburse the seller for the security deposit at closing. Both options have the same financial impact on you—the amount you will pay will be the same. You will simply need to work out how it will be paid.

If the seller has paid other security deposits, such as for an equipment lease, then you will pay the lessor or reimburse the seller in a similar manner.

Consent Fees

If the target business needs to get consent to transfer contracts to you, such as a lease, as part of the sale, the other parties to those contracts may require the payment of an administrative, consent, or transfer fee to process the request. This expense is most probable for the transfer of a lease. Many times, those fees, if they exist, are found in the language of the contract to be transferred. Even if the contract is silent on that issue, the other party might condition its consent on your payment of its administrative or attorney's fees associated with the request.

You can negotiate whether the seller will pay some or all of these fees.

Licenses and Government Approvals

You might need licenses to operate the target business after closing. For example, you might need a health department permit to operate a restaurant, an alcoholic beverage license to operate a bar, or a contractor's license to operate a construction company.

In Virginia, you also will need a business license to operate any business. All of these licenses require payment of a fee. You also might incur other indirect costs to get these licenses, such as paying for materials or a class to prepare you to take a test to obtain the license.

Insurance

You will want to obtain insurance to protect your business. If you are borrowing money to buy the business, then your lender most likely will require you to obtain insurance to protect the collateral that secures the loan. You will be required to pay the premium for the first year of insurance coverage up front, which will be an additional cost of buying and operating the business.

Broker's Commission

Brokers get paid a commission on the sale. The commission is calculated as a percentage of the purchase price. A customary broker's commission is 10%. The commission is paid at closing.

The broker typically represents the seller. Therefore, the seller is responsible for paying the broker's commission. At closing, the closing agent will collect the purchase price proceeds, then will disburse the broker's commission to the broker directly out of closing—i.e., that money never passes through the seller's hands.

If you retained a broker to help you find a business to buy, however, you might be responsible for paying your broker a fee or commission. The contract you have with your broker will indicate what the fee is and how and when it will get paid.

If two brokers are involved (one representing the seller and the other representing the buyer), then the brokers might agree to split the commission. The seller is obligated to pay to the seller's broker so that each broker gets a 5% commission. That split needs to be agreed upon by the brokers when you begin negotiations to buy the business.

Seller-Paid Closing Costs

The customary rule when buying a business is that the seller and the buyer pay their own closing costs. It has become common for the seller of a house to offer to pay some or all of the buyer's closing costs as an incentive to motivate the buyer to do the deal. This is not very common when buying a small business, however. It's the exception and doesn't happen very often.

Of course, you can ask the seller and your lender if they are willing to pay some or all of your additional costs. For example, a seller might agree to pay $1,000 toward your legal fees. If the seller or lender agrees to pay some of your costs, they usually will cap the amount they will pay and the type of costs they will cover.

Making yourself aware of the potential additional costs you will pay when you buy the business will help you calculate the true cost of buying the business. That knowledge also should reduce your stress associated with buying the business because you will avoid being surprised by additional costs after you have signed a binding contract to buy the target business.

CHAPTER 6

Financing the Purchase

You will need a lot of money to buy your target business. If you have enough cash to pay the purchase price and additional costs and expenses, then you do not need to read this chapter. Chances are, however, that you won't have the cash. You will need to look to other sources to help fund the purchase price and other costs.

Your Own Cash
Rarely is a buyer able to borrow 100% of the money needed to purchase a business. You might need as much as 10% to 20% of the purchase price and enough cash to cover the additional costs and expenses. You might have some money in savings, or you may think about liquidating assets such as a vehicle, boat, or a piece of real estate to raise the cash needed. Regardless of the source, you will need to have some cash on hand that you have not borrowed. This cash will be the "skin" you put in the game.

Investors
Once you have some of your own cash in hand, you will need to raise the balance from other sources. Outside investors are a potential source of money to purchase your target business. An outside investor

is someone who contributes money to a company you form in exchange for an equity ownership position in the new company. For example, if you form a corporation, you could sell stock to outside investors, allowing them to become part-owners of the new business.

Friends and Family Investors

> Jamie wanted to purchase a Cinnabon franchise for a local shopping mall. The total cost to purchase the franchise, lease the mall space, build out the leased space, buy the equipment, and operate the business until it was predicted to generate sufficient revenues was about $250,000. Jamie had a small percentage of that money in savings. He formed a corporation for the new business and then sold stock to some of his family members, long-standing friends, and former college roommates. He was able to raise all the money needed, and the investors enjoyed a return on their investment by sharing in the net revenues of the business as stockholders of the corporation.

There are laws that apply to bringing in investors, such as the Securities and Exchange Act of 1933 and your state's analogous securities act. These laws and their underlying regulations mandate everything from how you solicit your investors and what you are required to tell them about the investment to when and how to get government approval for the investment deal. What's the big deal about complying with securities laws? If you don't, you could be personally liable for refunding the investments to your investors and paying their attorney's fees.

Private Placement
One of the most popular ways to bring in outside investors is to conduct a "private placement." This deal takes advantage of an

exemption to the federal and state securities acts' requirement to get government approval of your investment deal. There are significant limitations on conducting a private placement, including:

- You cannot find investors through general solicitations or advertisements;
- You will not be allowed to post a plea on your website or an ad in a newspaper asking for investors; and
- You will be restricted to offering the investment deal to friends and family members.

In addition, the securities acts contain prohibitions against fraud that have resulted in customary practices about what types of documents you give your investors and what those documents say to protect you against securities fraud claims. The key document (sometimes called a "private placement letter" or a "private placement memorandum") should disclose:

- Key information about the business and your future plans and predictions;
- Risks associated with the business and investing in the company; and
- Customary disclosures about investments in general.

Complying with the securities laws' anti-fraud requirements for private placements is crucial because you could be personally liable for securities fraud claims, even if you have a corporation or limited liability company.

Some states also require registration of private placement deals. They have forms that need to be completed and filed along with fees to pay. Those states generally do not review and approve the private placement deal, but your deal needs to be on record with them to be valid. If you have potential investors in several states, you will need to comply with the securities act of each of those states. Compliance will require legal research of each state's securities act.

You may also borrow money from a private lender and give them a convertible promissory note. A convertible promissory note is a promise to repay the debt plus interest by a certain date. If you do not repay all of the debt and interest by that date, then the outstanding debt is converted into equity (e.g., stock in your corporation or membership interests in your limited liability company) based on a formula contained in the promissory note. Some promissory notes impose an automatic conversion, while others give the lender the option to convert. Under the federal and state securities laws, convertible promissory notes are considered "securities." As a result, borrowing money this way and issuing a convertible promissory note should be treated as a private placement.

The risks associated with private placements can be reduced if your investors are "accredited." The federal and state securities acts define the characteristics of an "accredited investor" based on the investor's net worth or annual income. The securities acts presume that an investor who has a considerable amount of assets or income should be in a better position and have more experience to evaluate the risks of an investment in a small business. Therefore, you won't have to comply with some of the private placement rules when you are dealing with an accredited investor.

While private placements are a common way to raise money to start or purchase a business, they involve risk. Your business lawyer can help you put together the private placement to decrease or avoid those risks. Note, however, that a private placement is a separate deal that will have legal fees and costs (e.g., filing fees) associated with it. You should factor those fees and costs into the total amount of money you need to raise from the private placement. For example, if the purchase price for your target business is $250,000 and you are going to raise $225,000 from a private placement (because you have $25,000 of your own cash), but the legal fees and costs involved with the private placement are estimated to be $10,000, then your private placement goal should be to raise $235,000 to cover those additional legal fees and costs.

There are other, more complicated ways to raise money from potential investors under the securities acts, but the costs usually are so high as to outweigh any potential benefit of using them to raise money for buying a small business.

Founder's Exemption
There is another commonly used exception to the securities laws for raising capital called the "founder's exemption." The founder's exemption implies that you already know the other founders and that you did not conduct any general solicitation or advertising to recruit founders. The founder's exemption is not contained in any language of the securities acts but is based on an implication and interpretation of those statutes. As a result, some lawyers take the position that the founder's exemption does not really exist. Nevertheless, use of and reliance on the founder's exemption is a widespread and common practice for raising money.

Rather than forming a company, then seeking potential investors for buying stock, the founder's exemption can apply when a group of individuals comes together to form a company for the purpose of starting a new business or buying an existing business. For example, if you and three friends decide to pool your money to form a company to buy a new business, then you can proceed without conducting a private placement or relying on any other type of securities law exemption.

The founder's exemption has some risk, too, because it doesn't appear in any statute or regulation. You can reduce that risk if you organize your founder's group before you start looking for a business to buy. You can further reduce that risk if your founder's group consists of people you already know—friends, family, and business acquaintances.

Crowdfunding
Crowdfunding has become a popular way to raise money for small businesses and projects. Crowdfunding typically consists of using a website platform, such as Kickstarter or Indiegogo, to advertise your project and solicit contributions or purchases from the general public. You cannot sell ownership in your business through crowdfunding, except in very limited circumstances. Instead, the creator of a crowdfunding campaign needs to provide its contributors with some other product, service, or premium in exchange for money.

Originally, the securities acts prohibited people from selling equity (e.g., stock in a corporation or membership interests in a limited liability company) by crowdfunding. The U.S. Securities and Exchange Commission adopted rules in 2015 to allow businesses to sell equity to investors through crowdfunding. To date, I have never had a client raise money this way. If you read the SEC's crowdfunding rules, you will understand why. The crowdfunding rules put so many severe restrictions on who can invest, how much they can invest, how much can be raised, where the crowdfunding campaign must be listed and managed, and what process needs to be followed that raising money by selling equity through crowdfunding is unattractive and time-consuming. You probably should consider a better use of your time rather than trying to sell equity through crowdfunding.

Another reason selling equity through crowdfunding is unattractive is the potential to end up with a lot of investors, many of whom you might not even know—so many that managing the business and being accountable to those investors might be overly burdensome. There might be ways to alleviate this problem, such as offering investors through crowdfunding only non-voting equity, but those limitations on the equity probably will turn off, rather than attract, potential investors.

Pros and Cons of Investors
However you do it, raising money from outside investors means bringing people into the business who will have some influence over its management and demand that you be accountable to them. The more investors you bring in, or the more money you raise from one investor, will correlate to the amount of control you give up in the business. Even if you keep a majority position in the company, outside investors contributing large amounts of money usually will negotiate some management authority and control in exchange for their investment. Think long and hard about bringing in investors, because it will be extremely difficult to get them to exit the business once they are in.

If you decide to raise money from outside investors, I suggest you curb your creativity about how you do it. The method for conducting a private placement has been around for a long time and is well-tested. Adopting a creative approach to bringing in investors that skirt the edges of the private placement rules is very risky. My experience is that people try to take shortcuts on private placements to increase the pool of potential investors. For example, they might engage in general solicitation for investors on the Internet. They do this to increase the likelihood that they will find enough investors (or a few investors with enough money) to meet their fundraising goal. However, they are taking a big risk because non-compliance with the securities laws can give a disgruntled investor the right to get his money back. In other words, creativity might increase the chances of losing your investment money and gaining a bad reputation in the local business community as someone who can't be trusted.

Trying to Entice Doctors and Dentists to Invest

Shannon and Betty founded a two-person independent film production company. For their first feature film, they conducted a customary private placement with some of their family members and friends and raised enough money to reach their fundraising goal. After filming and production had begun, however, the company realized it had not raised enough money to finish the project. As a result, Shannon and Betty had to contribute more money, most of which they borrowed as cash advances on their personal credit cards.

For their second feature film, they decided to approach investor recruitment differently to decrease the risk of underfunding and having to contribute additional personal money. They rented a trendy local restaurant that had a private room where the movie trailer could be screened. They invited a large number of potential investors, most of whom they had never met and did not know. Many of these potential investors were local doctors and dentists. They simply put the word out on the street about the project and asked friends and acquaintances to recruit people to attend the screening. When the potential investors arrived, they were given a copy of the private placement memorandum. The company founders then pitched the project and screened the trailer. The potential investors were asked to make a contribution in exchange for equity ownership before they left the restaurant.

This "creative" private placement approach was risky for several reasons. First, it could be argued that Shannon and Betty, "the founders," solicited potential investors in violation of the securities laws. Second, the founders did not give the potential investors a reasonable opportunity to read the private placement memorandum. Third, the founders did not give the potential investors a reasonable opportunity to have their advisers, such as an attorney or accountant, review and advise them on the private placement memorandum. As a result, the founders had traded the possibility of increasing their chances of funding their project for a greater risk that an investor might claim securities fraud and demand a refund of the investment.

In practicality, this fundraising approach did not work. The founders did not raise nearly enough money to fund the project. I believe their fundraising failure was due, in part, to their aggressive approach of requesting money at the end of the pitch. So, in the end, their creative approach backfired.

Remember that raising money from outside investors is an entirely separate deal from buying your new business. It adds another layer of significant risk to your project. This is not a deal to do on your own. You need to engage an experienced business lawyer to help you comply with the securities laws.

Loan

Most buyers borrow money to pay part of the purchase price. Borrowing money is a separate, additional deal. Your biggest challenge will be finding someone to loan the money to you.

Bank Loan

First, ask your bank if they are willing to loan you the money. Most banks have commercial lending departments that would be willing to take an application from you and review the deal. Commercial lending departments typically are reasonably quick at giving you a preliminary decision about whether they might be able to loan you the money.

If your bank is unwilling or unable to loan you the money, then check with other banks. Consider asking your team members (especially your business lawyer and accountant) whether they have any contacts at other banks to whom they can introduce you. Chances are your business lawyer has closed loans with many local banks and knows loan officers who would be interested in looking at your deal. Even if your team members do not have any contacts at local banks, they might know which local lenders customarily lend to small businesses.

A commercial lender will require you to secure the performance and payment of the loan by granting a lien to the lender on your business's assets and revenues so that it can foreclose on the business if you default on the loan. Most commercial lenders also will require you and your spouse to personally guarantee the loan. This gives the lender the ability to get to your personal assets, including your personal bank accounts and your home if you default on the loan. These terms and conditions to a commercial loan are customary.

In extreme situations, the lender may require additional collateral for the loan, such as a lien on other real estate you own.

Note that a commercial lender probably will not allow you to borrow the entire amount of the purchase price. Instead, they likely will be willing to loan you no more than 80% of the purchase price. You will need to come up with the other 20%.

Small Business Administration Loan
You may have heard of "SBA" or Small Business Administration loans and think they sound attractive and should be your most likely funding source. That's mostly a misconception. The SBA does not lend money directly to small businesses. Instead, local banks participate in SBA programs. The SBA guarantees the repayment of a percentage of the amount of the SBA loans made by the bank if you default.

The SBA loan guaranty gives the bank more incentive to lend to small businesses because it decreases the bank's risk. Additionally, the SBA loan might also allow the lender to loan you a higher percentage of the purchase price (e.g., 90%), thus decreasing the amount of money you will need to put into the deal personally. SBA loan programs have complex criteria for qualification, require more legal paperwork, and have more additional costs (you'll have to pay for the SBA guaranty) than traditional commercial loans. As a result, they should not be your first option for funding. Nevertheless, if you are interested in exploring the possibility of an SBA loan, you should ask around at local banks. There are likely several local banks in your area that originate SBA loans.

Line of Credit
Some people already have an existing line of credit, typically in the form of a second mortgage on their home. This is a loan that was made with the intent of providing you with a source of funding for your future. Some people use lines of credit to draw out equity from their home for home improvements, large purchases (such as a vehicle), or vacations. If you have a line of credit like that, then you might consider using it to fund as much of the purchase price as possible. Remember that your line of credit probably is secured by a lien on your house. Therefore, if you default on your line of credit, the lender could ultimately foreclose on your house.

Second Mortgage
Your house probably is your biggest asset. You might consider taking out a second mortgage on your home, if you have not already done so (e.g., for a line of credit). The possibility of getting a second mortgage will depend on many factors, including your credit rating and how much equity you have in your house. Your house will be the collateral for

the loan. The risk of using a second mortgage to fund part or all of the purchase price is the possibility of losing your home if you fail to pay back the loan.

Private Lender (Family or Friend)

You might also consider obtaining a loan from a private lender, such as a family member or close friend. For example, Billy needed a significant amount of money to purchase a healthcare practice. Even though he probably could have qualified for a loan from a commercial lender, his father-in-law had enough cash in savings and was willing to finance the purchase. The loan was documented as if it were a loan from a commercial lender. The "Applicable Federal Rate," set by the U.S. Government, was used as the interest rate for the loan. The result was that Billy was able to obtain a loan from a "friendly" lender, and his father-in-law benefited from the opportunity to earn interest income on his money.

Angel Lender

An angel lender is a private investor not in the lending business, but who is willing to make a loan to help a small business. I have documented and closed loans between business owners and wealthy private lenders, although this is a rare occurrence. Again, if you obtain this type of loan, the legal paperwork should be the same as if it were a loan from a commercial lender. Note, however, that borrowers usually get these types of loans because they cannot qualify for a commercial loan. As a result, the terms of a loan from a private lender (other than a friendly family member) probably will be less attractive than the terms you would otherwise get from a commercial lender, such as the interest rate being higher than what a bank would charge.

Hard Money Lender
In your search for financing, you might learn about "hard money lenders." Hard money lenders typically are private lenders who make short-term loans on terms much tougher than a commercial lender. Interest rates charged by hard money lenders usually will be much greater than interest rates charged by commercial lenders. You will also need to secure the loan with some collateral, such as the assets of the new business and perhaps some personal property—your home and vehicles, especially if they are paid for. Hard money lenders usually are less compromising and more difficult to work with than a commercial lender. They typically are more inclined to enforce their loans quickly if you default. Hard money loans should be your very last resort for financing, if you even consider them at all.

Cash Advance
Another potential source of funding might be a cash advance on your credit card. This is a loan from your credit card company. Although there is no collateral involved, you will be personally guaranteeing the loan based on the credit card terms and conditions you agreed to when the card was issued to you. The interest rate on credit card cash advances usually is so high that I do not recommend using cash advances as a source of funding unless you cannot get funding anywhere else and the amount you are borrowing is relatively low. Of course, the amount you can borrow

under a credit card typically has a cap. The amount you borrow also will decrease your available credit line under the card. Credit card advances are very unattractive for these reasons.

Retirement Benefits

Your retirement benefits also might be a source of funding. You might be able to borrow from your retirement accounts or roll over the money from your retirement account into your own business, rather than someone else's.

You typically can borrow money from your 401(k) or IRA retirement accounts. Those accounts already have terms and conditions for loans from them, including limits on how much you can borrow, the interest rate on the loan, when you have to start repaying the loan, and how long you will get to repay the loan. Loans from retirement accounts usually do not have the most favorable terms, but they probably will be a better source of financing than a credit card advance or a hard money lender.

You also might be able to roll over the money in your retirement account into a new corporate retirement account that will own your new business. Right now, the money you contribute to your retirement account is managed by a company which invests that money in publicly traded stocks and bonds. You may be able to create a new corporation and corporate retirement account and then roll over your existing retirement funds into the new corporate retirement account. The new corporate retirement account would then purchase the stock of your new corporation, rather than publicly traded corporations. As a result, the money in your retirement fund will be contributed to your new corporation as working capital to be used for purchasing your new business. Your retirement account will then be the owner of your new business, but it will be set up in a way that allows you to control the decisions for your business.

Rolling over your retirement investments in a new corporate retirement account is risky. The IRS considers these deals to be in a gray area of tax law. If the transaction is incorrectly done, then the IRS might tax you on the early withdrawal of your retirement funds and charge you an early withdrawal penalty. The tax rates on an early withdrawal can be very high.

There are financial advisers and lawyers who specialize in setting up these rollover deals to fund the purchase of a new business. The IRS has stringent rules that need to be followed to avoid inadvertently triggering the payment of significant taxes. For this reason, you need to engage a professional who understands the IRS rules and guidance on these types of transactions and has experience doing them. You might want to look for a professional who not only has the knowledge and experience of setting them up, but also has experience defending their existence to the IRS. Professionals likely will charge several thousand dollars to set up the rollover deal, which will be an added cost to buying your new business. As a result, financing your business purchase by rolling over your retirement fund may make sense only if you can access a large amount of cash in your existing retirement account.

Seller-Financing
The seller of the business might also agree to "loan" you a portion of the purchase price to close the deal. The seller won't give you money but may be willing to let you pay a portion of the purchase price over time.

If a seller agrees to finance a portion of the purchase price, you will pay a percentage of the purchase price to the seller at closing and then deliver a promissory note to the seller for the balance of the purchase price, plus interest. The promissory note will give you a period of time to pay the balance (e.g., 60 months), indicate the interest rate you will pay (which is usually equal to or slightly more than the rate you would pay a commercial lender), and indicate how often payments are to be made. You might pay equal monthly installments for the term of the promissory note, or you might make smaller monthly payments with one large final payment (a "balloon payment").

The seller will have a first position lien on the assets of the business. If you default on the promissory note, the seller will have the right to foreclose on the business and take back ownership so that it can operate the business, liquidate it, or sell it to someone else to recover losses.

The seller customarily will ask you and your spouse to personally guaranty the promissory note, as well. If you default on the promissory note, the seller will be able to foreclose on your personal assets, including your personal bank accounts and home, to collect.

Seller financing is customary, reasonable, and an attractive way to finance a portion of the purchase price. It is especially helpful if you are unable to get a commercial loan. But you will be asking the seller to take a big risk. That's why the seller will want a higher interest rate, the lien, and the personal guaranty.

Combinations

Funding the purchase price probably will require you to get funding from a combination of the above-described sources. Once you have your 10%–20% portion, you will need to look at other sources for the balance. Where you find the balance of the purchase price will depend on your circumstances. For example, if a commercial lender is willing to loan 50% of the purchase price, you might need to conduct a private placement to raise the balance of the purchase price.

Your personal financial circumstances will influence your funding sources.

- If you have a good credit rating and your target business has valuable assets and strong historical cash flow, a commercial lender might be willing to fund the balance.
- If you have close family members and friends who have cash to loan or invest, you may be able to fund the balance with a private placement or private loan.
- If you have a seller willing to finance the deal, then you should negotiate the terms of the promissory note and other related seller financing legal documents.
- If you have a retirement account and you are unable to obtain financing elsewhere, then you should consider exploring whether to borrow money from your retirement account or to roll your retirement funds over to a corporate retirement account that would purchase the business.
- You probably should not consider credit card cash advances or hard money loans, unless you have no other source of financing and the amount you will borrow will be relatively small. You typically do not want to borrow money from these sources because their interest rates are so high and the terms for repayment usually are harsh.

CHAPTER 7

WHAT ARE YOU BUYING?

When you buy a business, what are you really buying? There are two approaches to buying a business. First, you can buy the equity of the business. Second, you can buy the assets of the business. I'll explain the differences between these approaches and which one you should prefer.

Equity Deal

Your target business probably is owned and operated by an entity, such as a corporation or limited liability company. The owners of the entity actually own the equity of the entity—in the case of a corporation, stock; in the case of a limited liability company, membership interests.

In an equity deal, you buy the business by buying all of the stock or membership interests from the owners. You become the stockholder of the corporation or member of the limited liability company. By purchasing the stock, you become the owner of the entity, which, in turn, owns and controls all of the assets of the business.

When you buy all the equity in the business, you buy not only the business's assets but also all of its liabilities. If the business has debts, you become responsible for them after you buy the business. You also become responsible for all unknown liabilities the business might have. For example, if someone slipped and fell in the business before you bought it, but doesn't sue the business until after you bought it, then you will be responsible for that liability. If the business failed to pay some payroll taxes before you bought the business, but the taxing authority does not attempt to collect the taxes, civil penalties, and interest until after you bought the business, then you will be responsible for that, too.

Buyers usually avoid buying equity because they don't want to take on the risk of buying unknown liabilities. Yes, the Purchase Agreement can be drafted in a way to require the seller to pay for pre-closing, known liabilities. It also can be drafted to include a promise that the seller will reimburse the buyer or pay for unknown liabilities that arise after closing (called an "Indemnity"), but that promise is only as good as the seller's post-closing financial strength (i.e., if the seller has no money after closing, the promise is worthless because the buyer won't be able to collect on it). As a result, you should avoid buying the stock or membership interest of the business, unless you have a very good reason to do so.

If certain assets of the business cannot be transferred, your only option for buying the business may be to purchase the equity. For example, if the target business is a government contractor, the contracts with the federal government probably prohibit the transfer or assignment of the contracts to a new owner (you). Those contracts probably are some of the most valuable assets of the business (i.e., buying the business without getting those contracts would remove most, if not all of the value from your purchase). In this instance, buying the stock of the target business makes sense and may be the only way you can acquire the business with the government contracts. You still will be taking on the risk of buying the known and unknown liabilities of the business, but obtaining the valuable government contracts probably outweighs that risk.

Equity deals are the exception, rather than the norm, for purchasing a small business. They are the least attractive approach from a buyer's perspective because of the significant risk. As a result, you always should push for an asset deal when buying a business.

Asset Deal

Every viable business has assets. These assets are the source of value for the business. A business's assets may include the office furniture and equipment; machinery; raw materials; work-in-progress and finished product; inventory; contracts with customers, vendors, or suppliers; license agreements; cash on hand; vehicles; supplies; tools; advertising; and signage. These types of assets are called "tangible" assets because you can touch, hold, and see them.

A business's assets also include valuable assets you cannot touch, hold, and see. These are referred to as "intangible" assets, and also are quite valuable. In fact, the intangible assets probably will be the most valuable assets you acquire. Intangible assets include trademarks (brands), copyrights, the "good will" or reputation of the business, phone numbers, domain names, and website content.

Buying a business as an asset deal allows you to purchase most of the business's assets while leaving the seller responsible for the liabilities associated with the operation of the business before closing (the date on which the business is transferred to you). The sale of the assets will separate them from the seller's liabilities, making an asset deal not as risky as an equity deal because you are not exposing yourself to buying unknown business liabilities. In an asset deal, those liabilities remain with the seller.

Asset deals are by far the best choice for a buyer when buying a business. Equity deals should be considered only when an asset deal is not possible. It is important to know and understand the differences between an equity and asset deal because some sellers (and their brokers) may subtly try to draw you into an equity deal to shift responsibility for known and unknown liabilities. They may begin negotiations with talk about buying the business, and you may not realize they intend to do an equity deal until you see the contract. Even then, you need to pay close attention to how the contract is drafted to be sure you are buying only assets and those selected liabilities which you agree to take on, if any.

Real Estate

If your target business has a physical location, it either owns or rents the space. If you want the business to remain in that space after closing, you will need to determine whether you will buy or rent the space as part of the business acquisition. If you don't buy or rent the real estate, you will need to move the business into another physical location after closing, so you might need to buy or rent another location unless you already own property where you can locate the business.

Buying the location is possible only if the seller owns the real estate (e.g., the building or office condo). If the seller does not own the real estate, or if it will retain ownership of the real estate, then you will need to lease the location from whoever owns it.

Buying or leasing real estate is a separate deal from buying the business, although the lines between the deals might get blurry if the seller of the business also is the seller or landlord of the real estate. The Purchase Agreement for the business should indicate what will happen, but you also will need a separate contract (e.g., a real estate purchase agreement or a lease) to handle the real estate deal.

Liabilities

Even if you avoid an equity deal and buy assets, you probably will end up buying some of the target business's liabilities. Liabilities include things such as debt owed on a line of credit the seller uses for advances to cover payroll; accounts payable for normal expenses incurred in the course of operating the business; accrued, but unpaid taxes; rent; and amounts owed to vendors or suppliers for purchased materials. If these liabilities are incurred prior to closing but do not become due until after closing, make sure your Purchase Agreement assigns responsibility to the appropriate party.

It is fair, customary, and reasonable that the seller pays for liabilities it incurred before closing, even if they don't become due until after closing. For that reason, make sure the Purchase Agreement clearly indicates that the seller will be responsible for those liabilities. In fact, you'll want to require that the seller disburse the proceeds received at closing for the purchase price directly to its creditors to pay off the business's liabilities.

Because the seller retains most, if not all, the liabilities, it also is fair, customary, and reasonable that the seller retains the uncollected accounts receivables, even if those receivables won't be collected until after closing. Those accounts receivables are related to work performed or product sold by the seller prior to closing and are assets of the business. They are customarily retained by the seller and excluded from the sale of the business.

What liabilities usually are transferred to a buyer in an asset sale? Typically, they are liabilities associated with contracts that are being sold to the buyer as part of the business. For example, if the seller has a lease for its location, the buyer may agree to become the tenant under the lease, and have the lease and its obligations transferred to the buyer. In addition, if the seller has entered into contracts with customers that will be fulfilled after closing, then the buyer will want those contracts transferred to it and will become responsible for performing them. Note, however, that even in these instances, you want to assume responsibility only for liabilities arising under these contracts **after** closing. You'll want the Purchase Agreement to indicate that the seller will be responsible for those liabilities before closing and also promise that it will reimburse you for any money you have to pay out under those contracts for liabilities incurred before closing.

Make sure both you and the seller clearly understand what you are buying and what the seller is keeping.

As a buyer, you want to do an asset deal and assume as few liabilities as possible. You also want to make sure that your seller remains responsible for all liabilities arising prior to closing, even if you are assuming some of them. Your Purchase Agreement needs to cover these issues in detail so that you will be able to resolve any dispute about what you have purchased and who is responsible for which liabilities.

CHAPTER 8

Before You Sign the Purchase Agreement

Now that you have found a target business to buy, determined how to finance the purchase, and set the deal up as an asset purchase, it is time to do some homework before signing the Purchase Agreement. This is the time to acquire more detailed information about the target business and the seller and verbally negotiate the most significant terms of the deal. In addition, you and the seller might decide to enter into a letter of intent to take the business off the market and allow for more negotiation time.

Ask Probing Preliminary Questions
Get to know the seller and the target business by asking probing questions about the business. Some important questions include:

- How long has the business been open and operating?

- What is the financial track record of the business (i.e., has the business been losing money, remaining steady, or growing)?

- What are the reasons driving the track record?
  For example, if the business has been shrinking, is it because the owner is nearing retirement and has slowed down? Or perhaps she is suffering from a health challenge? Or, if the business has been growing, what has propelled that growth (e.g., a key employee who might leave soon, an upturn in the economy, a newly acquired key customer)?

- Did the owner found the business or did she buy it from someone else?
  If the owner is the founder of the business, that might indicate that the owner truly is the business and that the value of the business might suffer significantly once she is no longer involved.

- Why is the owner selling?
  The seller may not give a straight answer to this question, but you need to ask it and probe some. The seller's answer also will help evaluate her credibility. If you discover in your review of the books and records that the state of the business tells a story different than the seller's reasons for selling, you can gauge how much you can trust the seller during negotiations.

- Are there other potential buyers for the business?
  The answer to this question might help you understand the level of the seller's motivation to sell. If you are the only buyer, you might have more leverage in the negotiations.

- How long has the business been for sale?
  Again, the answer to this question might help determine how much leverage you have. If the business has been on the market for a long time and you are the only buyer, the seller might be more inclined to agree to your terms because she might be getting increasingly anxious or desperate to sell the business.

Informally gathering information about the seller and the business at the beginning of the negotiation process will help identify any "red flags" with the deal. If the business has been on the market for a long time and there have been other potential buyers who have passed on the deal, that might indicate that the seller is very difficult to negotiate with, that the business is overvalued, or that the business has problems that seriously jeopardize its potential for success. Identifying red flags might result in your walking away from the deal or may help you develop a strategy for moving forward with negotiations to purchase the business on more reasonable terms.

Visit the Business

Go see what you might be buying. If the business has a physical location, go on a site visit. Walk around the facility, see the equipment, inspect the vehicles, see how the employees do their jobs, and do a preliminary assessment of the business. A site visit should be done only with the seller's permission, and the owner should accompany you during the visit.

Be extra careful not to disclose the purpose of your visit to anyone, other than the owner, because the owner may not have told his employees that he is considering selling the business. **This is critical!** I have been involved in deals where the seller's employees discovered that the business was up for sale because they overheard the potential buyer say something during the site visit. Those employees then became upset and threatened to quit. This becomes a big problem for both the seller and the buyer because if the employees quit before closing, then the buyer might be left in a bad position where he will have to find and train new employees as soon as he buys the business. The seller also might be put in a bad position, especially if the deal does not close, because business operations might suffer due to possible employee exits. A good practice to protect against inadvertent disclosure is to jot down any questions you develop during your site visit and discuss them with the owner later in a confidential setting.

Negotiate Significant Terms
Before you sign a Purchase Agreement is the time to negotiate the significant terms of the purchase. From a buyer's perspective pin down:

- What you are buying;

- Which assets you will get;

- Which assets the seller will keep;

- Which liabilities you will take on (e.g., lease, customer contracts);

- What you will pay for the business (this may include not only the purchase price for the assets but also compensation for a non-competition restriction and post-closing consulting services from the seller);

- How the purchase price was determined;

- How you will pay the purchase price (e.g., will you make a down payment and pay installments over time under a promissory note? Will a portion of the purchase price be contingent on meeting certain conditions, such as revenues hitting certain levels?); and

- What type of transition assistance you will get from the seller (e.g., will the seller provide any training? Will the seller introduce you to customers, vendors, suppliers, subcontractors, etc.? Will the seller be available after the closing to answer questions about running the business? If the seller will provide assistance, how much will it cost?)

The answers to these questions will help you develop an outline for the structure of the deal that will form the basis for drafting the Purchase Agreement.

Letter of Intent

Some buyers and sellers like to get "engaged" before they get "married." Entering into a **non-binding** letter of intent is similar to getting engaged. Signing a **binding** Purchase Agreement is like getting married.

A Letter of Intent is a written document that describes the significant terms of the deal. Customarily, it is non-binding, except for the few provisions explained below. In other words, a Letter of Intent does not obligate the buyer to buy the business or the seller to sell the business.

The Letter of Intent expresses the intent of the buyer and seller to enter into a deal. It should contain significant terms, such as a brief description of the assets to be purchased, the purchase price, and the payment terms. It also may contain a potential closing date. The Letter of Intent should also give the buyer the exclusive right to purchase the business for a limited period and require the seller to deal exclusively with the buyer during that period. It also may give the buyer a period to review the business's books and records, tax returns, physical location, equipment, inventory, and other assets of the business.

The Letter of Intent usually is not a binding contract, although it should contain several provisions that are binding. The parts of the Letter of Intent that should be binding include:

- A promise that each party will keep confidential information it receives or reviews from the other party;
- The seller's promise that it will not deal with anyone other than the buyer about the sale of the business for a limited period of time—i.e., a promise to take the target business off the market;
- The seller's promise to allow the buyer to inspect the business; and
- The buyer's promise to reimburse the seller for any damages or losses arising out of the buyer's inspection of the business.

Be careful about how the Letter of Intent is drafted, if you use one. Use your business lawyer to draft and review any Letter of Intent you are considering to protect your interests and reduce the risk of making mistakes.

Purchase Agreement Disguised as Letter of Intent

Emma brought a "Letter of Intent," drafted by the seller's broker, to her business lawyer. It contained the essential terms of the deal, but nowhere in the Letter of Intent did it say that it was non-binding. As a result, had Emma signed the Letter of Intent, she probably would have entered into a binding contract to purchase the business on the terms and conditions contained in the Letter of Intent without any opportunity to negotiate the deal. That is not what Emma wanted, and her business lawyer saved her from that potentially disastrous outcome by realizing and pointing out that the so-called "Letter of Intent," was really a Purchase Agreement.

Most buyers and sellers of small businesses do not use Letters of Intent, however. They avoid them because they typically do not want to spend the time or incur the legal fees associated with creating a Letter of Intent. Usually, they also have developed a certain amount of trust with each other on which they will rely during the period before they sign a binding Purchase Agreement.

Confidentiality or Nondisclosure Agreement

Instead of entering into a Letter of Intent, some buyers and sellers sign a Confidentiality or Nondisclosure Agreement (different names for the same type of contract) before sharing information about the target business and the buyer. A Confidentiality or Nondisclosure Agreement is a binding contract that defines what confidential information is and puts limits on what the party receiving the confidential information can do with it. Limitations include using it only for the purpose of evaluating the proposed deal and requiring the return or destruction of the other person's confidential information if either the buyer or seller decides not to do the deal.

A seller usually is more interested in having a Confidentiality Agreement than a buyer because the seller typically is turning over lots of confidential information about the business. Because the buyer probably is not disclosing confidential information, the buyer should not initiate the idea of a Confidentiality Agreement. It is customary and reasonable for a seller to ask for a Confidentiality Agreement, however, so the buyer should not push back against that request. From a buyer's perspective, a Confidentiality Agreement is a good idea if the seller is reluctant to turn over information about the business for your evaluation (especially if the buyer and the seller are competitors) because it might ease the seller's concerns. You should have your business lawyer look over any proposed Confidentiality Agreement before you sign it because it is a binding legal contract and you want to make sure it is customary and reasonable.

Most buyers and sellers do not use Confidentiality Agreements, however. Perhaps they just are not aware they exist, or maybe they don't want to spend the time and legal fees of putting one together. If the parties decide to use a Confidentiality Agreement, legal fees should be quite low because it's not a complicated contract and a business lawyer should already have a template as a good starting point. In most instances, however, buyers and sellers simply rely on the trust they have established or decide not to turn over confidential information until after they have signed a binding Purchase Agreement, which customarily contains confidentiality restrictions.

Getting as much information about the business before you sign a binding Purchase Agreement will help you assess and manage potential risks. If the information paints a bad picture, then it may be enough to help you decide not to enter into the deal. If the information is positive and encouraging, it might strengthen your confidence about your decision to buy the business. For these reasons, you will find that your research before signing a contract will be valuable and might help as you consider your strategy for negotiating the Purchase Agreement.

CHAPTER 9

IS IT A GOOD DEAL?

How can you decide whether buying the target business is a good deal? You'll not only need information about the business, but you'll need to know how to decipher that information or to hire someone that can.

Usually, there is not a lot of public information available about a small business. Most of the information obtained will be from the business itself. The preliminary information you obtained from the business will help you decide whether to sign a binding Purchase Agreement, but you should keep researching the business after you have signed the agreement to decide whether to close on the purchase.

In Chapter 11, I describe the anatomy of a Purchase Agreement, but for now, I assume your capable business lawyer has negotiated into the Purchase Agreement the right for you to conduct "due diligence." Due diligence allows for an inspection for a limited period of time and the right to terminate the Purchase Agreement if something is discovered about the business that isn't acceptable.

Dig deeper into the business during the due diligence period. The information found during the due diligence period will help you make the final decision about whether the business is a good buy.

Rely on your team to help find and interpret the information. Your team members should know which questions to ask, which information to look for, and what the information indicates about the business. Some of your team members, such as your business lawyer, may have a checklist you can use to guide you through your due diligence efforts.

At a minimum, your team should look at the following items during the due diligence period:

> Lien and Judgment Search—your business lawyer should engage a search company to search public records to determine if there are any recorded liens or judgments against the business or its assets. One reason to do this search is to identify all the liens the seller will pay off at closing. This needs to happen so you don't take ownership of an asset with a lien on it and become responsible for paying that lien or chasing down a seller after closing to pay the lien or reimburse you for your payment. In addition, you don't want to risk buying an asset that could be taken from you through foreclosure.
>
> Also, if you are borrowing money to buy the business, your lender will want to record a lien against the assets as collateral. The lender will not allow another lien against the assets to exist because an existing lien would trump your lender's lien, giving the seller's creditor the right to foreclose on the asset. As a result, your lender would have no security.
>
> Another reason to conduct the lien search is to get an idea of whether the business is in any trouble. For example, if you find vendors, creditors, contractors, or tax agencies have filed liens or obtained judgments against the business,

you should investigate why the business was unable to pay its debts and expenses when they came due. That investigation might uncover some reasons that make buying the business less attractive to you.

Financial Information—look at all the business's financial information, including a complete copy of its bookkeeping and accounting records (e.g., get a copy of its QuickBooks data).

Reviewing profit and loss statements, both current and historical, and a balance sheet are essential in obtaining an overview of the business's financial situation. Dig deep into the details of any line items on the financial statements that appear out-of-the-ordinary.

Review the past three to five years of tax returns. If the business has been audited by a government agency (e.g., IRS, state tax department, or state labor department), you should review the audit and the business's responses and corrections.

I strongly recommend you engage the accountant on your team to help you review and interpret the financial information because her experience and training might identify issues you won't see.

Significant Contracts —acquire copies of and review all of the significant contracts that you'll be buying.

- If you are assuming a lease, you need to review it.
- If you are buying contracts with ongoing customers, you need to review them.

- If the business has important, mission critical contracts with vendors that you will be buying (e.g. enterprise-wide software license), you need to review them.
- If you are buying a franchised business, you need to review the Uniform Franchise Offering Circular and the franchise agreement.

During your review, look for:

- Negative contract provisions that might be applied to you (e.g., harsh rent escalation or fee escalation clauses);
- Limitations on the transfer of the contracts, such as consents required by the other party to the contract and fees that might be charged for transferring the contract; and
- Provisions that explain the mechanics for transferring the contract.

Understand the terms and conditions of the contracts to determine whether you might be taking on any unwanted obligations or liabilities. Review the contracts to determine whether they match the value the seller has placed on them as part of the basis for the purchase price. You also want to review the contracts to determine whether the other party might have the right to terminate a contract shortly after closing because you don't want to pay for something that you could lose shortly after buying the business.

I strongly recommend engaging a business lawyer to help review the contracts because his experience and training might identify issues that would not be apparent to a buyer.

Employees and Independent Contractors—You will want to take a close look at the employees of the business for at least two reasons. First, to make sure the business has complied with wage and hour laws to assure you aren't taking on a potential claim for the seller's pre-closing violations. Second, to evaluate the workforce to determine whom you might keep and whom you might let go after closing.

Determine whether any of the employees and independent contractors have written employment or independent contractor agreements, non-competition contracts, intellectual property rights ownership agreements, or confidentiality agreements with the business. Review those contracts to understand the obligations you will be taking on, what rights the business has under those agreements, and whether the contracts are enforceable.

Non-competition agreements and non-competition provisions in employment agreements are tricky. If they are not drafted correctly, they will be unenforceable. This is an important determination to make because you don't want to get into a situation where you have purchased the business, but a key employee with an unenforceable non-competition restriction quits and gains employment with a competitor.

Employees who do not have any written contracts with the business probably will have the right to leave the business anytime, including just before or after you buy the business. Likewise, you might have the right to terminate any of those employees for any reason (other than a reason against the law, such as discrimination) after you buy the business.

Equipment—Are you buying any equipment that has a title associated with it, such as a truck or trailer? If so, review copies of the titles to look for any liens or abnormalities. Confirm that the business owns the title(s). For example, if the business claims to own a vehicle, but cannot produce the title, that's a red flag issue that needs to be understood, and, if possible, resolved. Inspect the equipment to determine whether it might need to be repaired or replaced soon. You'll probably not want to buy 10 out-of-date computers that will need to be replaced soon after you buy the business.

Environmental Issues—Determine whether the business poses any potential environmental risks. Investigation into environmental concerns will be triggered by the business's industry. For example, you probably don't need to be concerned about or investigate environmental issues if you are buying a software development business. On the other hand, if you are buying a convenience store that sells gasoline, you need to investigate the property for potential environmental issues, such as leaking underground storage tanks or past spills.

You will become liable for past environmental problems when you buy the business, even if they arose from incidents occurring before you owned the business. Knowing about potential environmental problems before you buy the business will help you decide whether to buy the business and, if so, how to negotiate to get the seller to fix the environmental issues before closing. The seller also should promise to pay for any losses or damages suffered after closing as a result of those problems.

Do not try to identify environmental problems by yourself. Engage an environmental engineering company to perform a site assessment of the business (typically called a "Phase I Environmental Site Assessment"). The environmental engineer will produce a written report containing her observations from her site visit and historical information found in public records about any environmental incidents or conditions reported on the business property. The engineer also may recommend additional investigation, including soil testing and groundwater testing (typically called a "Phase II Environmental Investigation"), if the Phase I Environmental Site Assessment discovers significant potential environmental problems. A strong recommendation for a Phase II investigation will probably be a showstopper for you because the magnitude of the potential problem and the liability associated with it likely will be so much greater and more expensive to fix than the business is worth.

Intellectual Property—A significant amount of the value of some businesses comes from their intellectual property rights. Intellectual property rights include trademark rights (i.e., brand recognition and good will), copyrights (e.g., for software, written materials, photographs, music, etc.), trade secrets (the "secret sauce," the "secret recipes," the confidential know-how about running the business, making the products, or providing the services), and patents (e.g., inventions the business owns). If you are buying a business whose value is based on intellectual property rights, investigate those rights to make sure the seller owns them, that they do not infringe on anyone else's intellectual property rights, and that no one is infringing on the seller's intellectual property rights.

Check the public records of any patents or trademarks registered with the U.S. Patent & Trademark Office or the state trademark office. The Patent & Trademark Office's online databases for patents and trademarks can be found at www.uspto.gov. Check the public records of any copyrights registered with the U.S. Copyright Office. The Copyright Office's online database of registered copyrights can be found at www.copyright.gov. While you can check these databases yourself, I suggest having your business lawyer search the databases and interpret the data for you, assuming the business lawyer is familiar with intellectual property rights and how to protect them.

Trade secrets cannot be registered, so no database of trade secrets exists. Instead, make sure the business has reasonable practices and procedures in place to protect its trade secrets, such as confidentiality agreements with its employees and independent contractors.

Check written agreements with independent contractors and employees and the employee handbook (or individual employee policies) to determine whether the business has adequately documented that any intellectual property developed by an employee or independent contractor is owned by the business. Many times, those agreements are poorly drafted and do not properly transfer the intellectual property rights to the business, especially in the case of independent contractors. Have a business lawyer review these documents who knows intellectual property law well and is experienced in drafting and interpreting documents related to intellectual property rights. Avoid buying a business that cannot show how it obtained intellectual property rights.

Finally, if the business licenses intellectual property rights from others (e.g., mission-critical software) or licenses its intellectual property rights out to others (e.g., software or brand names), then review those licenses and the business's relationship with its licensor or licensee to determine whether the licenses are properly drafted and enforceable.

Due diligence investigation after signing the Purchase Agreement is necessary to give you a deeper, more thorough look at the business to evaluate whether you want to buy it. Your investigation may lead you to terminate the deal to avoid significant risks. If you fail to investigate the target business thoroughly, you might end up buying a business that has significant liabilities or assets that have little to no value. Either way, you will have made a bad deal and set yourself up for certain failure.

CHAPTER 10

PURCHASE AGREEMENT DRAFTING PROBLEMS

The Purchase Agreement you sign with the seller will become the binding legal document that will control your deal. It also will be the legal document to which everyone will look to resolve disputes that arise after you buy the target business. If the Purchase Agreement is well-drafted, then you will minimize the risk of legal disputes and maximize the possibility of clear and fair resolutions of disputes. A well-drafted Purchase Agreement will provide certainty and predictability.

The buyer and the seller often have negotiated all of the significant terms of the deal verbally before they put them in writing in a Purchase Agreement. As a result, the buyer and seller often view the Purchase Agreement as a mere formality. This causes the buyer and seller to downplay the Purchase Agreement, which could set them up for problems later.

The general problems I describe below many times spring from the buyer's and the seller's decision to take shortcuts when drafting the Purchase Agreement. Why would a buyer or seller want to take shortcuts in a deal? Sometimes, the parties believe the shortcuts will save on legal fees; other times, they believe the deal is friendly and that a detailed contract is not necessary; and still other times, the parties take shortcuts because they believe that drafting and negotiating a contract will take too much time, especially if lawyers are involved.

With those thoughts in mind, I want you to know that **shortcuts create risk for you**, the buyer.

Your business lawyer and you should be on the lookout for certain problems with the Purchase Agreement before you sign it. These problems include using a template that doesn't fit the deal, ambiguity in the contract, undefined words, agreements to agree, and verbal agreements not reflected in writing. I explain each of these potential problems below.

Bad Templates—One-Size-Fits-All Forms

Buyers and sellers use template or form Purchase Agreements because they believe it will help them save on legal fees. You can find examples of Purchase Agreements online. Online companies also sell form Purchase Agreements. In addition, if a broker is involved in the deal, he probably has a form Purchase Agreement he would like everyone to use. Many buyers and sellers believe they can simply print up one of these templates, fill in the blanks, and move forward.

Misuse of Templates Make Bad Deals

Art wanted to buy a business. He met with me to review a document he said was a "non-binding letter of intent." The document was a broker's template Purchase Agreement.

Had Art signed the document, he would have entered into a binding contract to buy the business on the terms and conditions in the broker's template agreement without any chance to negotiate those terms or to determine whether they fit the deal.

That's the biggest problem with using a template; it doesn't fit the deal. It usually leaves out important aspects of your particular deal, which means that the binding contract you signed does not contain the same deal you verbally negotiated. Then you will be stuck with what the written Purchase Agreement says about the deal.

Another problem with a template pulled from the Internet or provided by a broker is that you have no idea how up-to-date the contract is. Online templates and broker agreements may have been drafted many years ago. Outdated templates may not comply with current law. In addition, an outdated template might fail to address circumstances that didn't exist when the template was drafted. For example, the template might fail to transfer intellectual property rights properly, which would leave a large hole in your deal if those rights make up a valuable portion of the business.

In addition, Purchase Agreements are governed by state law. A template you find online that was drafted for use in another state might have provisions that are unenforceable in your state or may be enforced or interpreted differently.

Some buyers and sellers also believe they can save on legal fees by drafting the Purchase Agreement with a template and then having their business lawyer review and tweak it.

Re-Drafting Costs Money, Too

Olivia was selling a retail store. She agreed for the buyer to put together a Purchase Agreement using an online Purchase Agreement form. Olivia brought the template Purchase Agreement to me for a "quick review." Because the contract was so poorly drafted, I had to start over from scratch. Olivia spent more legal fees taking this approach than she would have spent had she simply asked me to draft a Purchase Agreement.

Your business lawyer will have her own starting point for drafting an asset Purchase Agreement—her own particular template if you will. But your business lawyer's template should be much better than anything you find online or get from a broker because your business lawyer is a licensed professional and has refined and updated her template from years of doing deals. When your business lawyer uses her template as the starting point, you get the benefit of all of her experience from previous deals without having to pay legal fees for it.

Even if the seller's business lawyer drafts the Purchase Agreement, you still will get the benefit of starting with a contract drafted by a lawyer. Your business lawyer's review of that agreement should not require a significant re-writing of the contract. Instead, your business lawyer will be more focused on making sure the Purchase Agreement reflects your understanding of the terms of the deal and contains customary and reasonable protections for you, as the buyer.

You will avoid the risk of having provisions of your contract be unenforceable if a business lawyer (whether yours or the seller's) drafts the Purchase Agreement. That peace of mind and time saved are well worth the legal fees you will pay.

Ambiguity

You want to be able to look to the Purchase Agreement for answers to help you resolve any dispute that arises between the seller and you. If the contract is ambiguous, then you will not be able to resolve the dispute without a lawsuit or arbitration. Lawsuits and arbitrations cost a lot of money and time, and the outcome always is uncertain.

Ambiguity means not only that a word or phrase is unclear, but also that a word or phrase might be subject to multiple interpretations. For example, the term "monthly payments" in a contract can have multiple meanings without further explanation. What day are the payments due? Are the payments to be equal, or is any payment during a month satisfactory? What do the payments consist of (e.g., interest only, principal only, or principal and interest)? Clarity helps avoid disputes.

Ambiguous words and phrases in contracts probably won't be enforceable. Additionally, if you go to court to ask a judge to provide an interpretation of or meaning to ambiguous words and phrases, state law might prohibit a judge from considering conversations or correspondence you had about the meaning of those words and phrases. In that instance, you will be stuck with a contract that does not reflect the deal you thought you struck.

Your perspective of whether a contract is clear versus ambiguous may not match the seller's perspective. In addition, what you consider unambiguous, might still be unclear under the law. My local law library has a book entitled, *Words and Phrases*. This thick book contains a collection of definitions and interpretations Virginia courts have adopted during lawsuits where parties to contracts have asked the court to clear up ambiguous contract language. Remember that the courts may not define or interpret words and phrases the same way you do.

Capturing understandings in writing can be difficult. You may believe that the parties "know what they mean," but when a dispute arises, the contract language will be scrutinized and picked apart to support each side's position. Your business lawyer should be able to review the Purchase Agreement to identify and correct ambiguous words and phrases to help reduce this risk.

Undefined Words

Poorly drafted Purchase Agreements often include keywords that are not defined. Undefined words are another form of ambiguity. For example, the contract may refer to the "Property," the "Assets," or the "Contracts," but fail to define what those terms mean by giving an address for the property, including a list of the assets, or including a list of the contracts. Failing to define keywords opens the door to additional ambiguity in the contract.

This problem can be cured by including definitions in the contract for keywords. Your business lawyer should be able to pick out the undefined keywords and draft definitions for them. Doing so will strengthen the enforceability of the Purchase Agreement and help avoid disputes or resolve them quickly by referring to clear contract language.

Agreements to Agree

Buyers and sellers often have difficulty agreeing on all the terms of the purchase. One way they try to move forward without resolving an issue is to put language in the Purchase Agreement indicating that they will agree upon a resolution in the future. For example, if the seller will work as an independent contractor for the buyer after closing to help with the transition of the business, but the parties cannot agree on how much compensation to pay the seller for her services, the buyer and seller might put a provision in the Purchase Agreement to indicate that the parties will determine the compensation at a later date. This is an agreement to agree.

Agreements to agree are unenforceable in my state and may be unenforceable in your state. This means that putting an agreement to agree provision in a contract is equivalent to leaving that provision out of the contract. A Virginia court will not force one party to agree with another party because the contract lacks details about what the agreement should be. In my example above, for instance, how would a court force one party to agree with the other party on the amount of compensation when the parties have provided no details about how to set or measure that compensation? Courts in Virginia will not write or rewrite the contract for you.

Your business lawyer should be able to identify agreements to agree and correct them. Of course, one way to correct them is to get the parties to agree on the terms while drafting the contract, and then draft those specific terms into the contract. Another way to correct agreements to agree may be to have the parties agree to adopt a method for making the decision later, such as adopting a formula containing agreed upon criteria. As a last resort, you might consider imposing upon each party a contractual obligation to negotiate in good faith for a limited period and then have the

Purchase Agreement indicate what will happen if the parties cannot come to an agreement during that limited time period.

Verbal Agreements Not in the Contract

Buyers and sellers often attempt to cure any ambiguity in the Purchase Agreement by referring to verbal agreements they reached during the negotiation process. Unfortunately, those verbal agreements probably become unenforceable once the Purchase Agreement is signed. As explained above, a court probably will not consider those verbal agreements if the parties ask the court to interpret and enforce the written Purchase Agreement.

An example of an unenforceable verbal agreement is a representation by the seller about the condition of an asset or the business. If the seller verbally promises the buyer that a piece of machinery is in good working order, but the written purchase fails to include that promise, then the promise is unenforceable. This means that you will be stuck with repairing the machine if it is broken when you buy it.

A well-drafted Purchase Agreement also will contain a "merger clause." This paragraph usually is entitled, "Entire Agreement." It is found near the end of the Purchase Agreement in what people often refer to as a set of paragraphs that make up the "boilerplate" provisions of the contract (see Chapter 11). The merger clause clearly indicates that the written agreement contains the entire agreement between the parties and supersedes all verbal agreements and promises made before closing. The merger clause strengthens the concept that verbal agreements not contained in the Purchase Agreement are unenforceable.

Tell your business lawyer everything about the deal you have negotiated so that she can ensure that all verbal agreements have been properly memorialized in the written Purchase Agreement. Review the draft Purchase Agreement, as well, to determine whether the verbal agreements have been included. Once the Purchase Agreement is signed, there will not be another chance to include verbal agreements into the contract, unless the seller will agree to a written amendment to the Purchase Agreement to include those missing verbal agreements. This may create a negotiation advantage for the seller because she might not be willing to agree to changes unless you are willing to give up something the seller wants.

Making sure your Purchase Agreement is clear and enforceable will protect you against risks you did not agree to assume. It also will strengthen the enforceability of the contract. If a dispute arises, a clear and enforceable Purchase Agreement should help you resolve the dispute because you will be able to rely on the contract language to tell you who is responsible for what.

CHAPTER 11

Anatomy of a Purchase Agreement

The Purchase Agreement is the controlling legal document for your deal. It should clearly describe the terms of the deal and allocate the risks between the buyer and the seller. It also will be the basis for resolving any disputes between the buyer and the seller. It needs to be well-drafted, and you need to understand what it says.

The Purchase Agreement will be full of legal words, phrases, and concepts. Many people stress about the Purchase Agreement because they don't understand what it says. They complain about the "legalese" or legal words and definitions.

Below, I am going to describe to you the most common words, phrases, and concepts found in a typical Purchase Agreement. This will help you understand the Purchase Agreement and arm you with enough knowledge to ask your business lawyer good questions in order to increase your understanding and tailor the Purchase Agreement to your unique deal.

The following descriptions are based on an assumption that you will sign the Purchase Agreement on one date, and then close the deal on a different date in the future. This approach to buying a business is similar to the approach you may have experienced if you have purchased a house. In that instance, you signed the sales contract weeks or months before actually closing on and getting title to the house. The sales contract contained provisions that governed the time period between signing the contract and closing on the purchase. Asset purchases of businesses also can proceed in the same way.

Many businesses are purchased using an approach where the parties sign the Purchase Agreement and close the deal (i.e., transfer title to the assets) on the same day. This approach is referred to as a "simultaneous" signing and closing. Because there is no time period between signing and closing, some of the provisions described below are not necessary or should be changed in the Purchase Agreement to reflect a simultaneous signing and closing. A section at the end of this chapter explains how you might change the Purchase Agreement for a simultaneous signing and closing.

This chapter is long because Purchase Agreements cover a lot of material. There is great value in reading this entire chapter, of course, but I suggest using this chapter as a reference to help when reviewing the Purchase Agreement for your deal.

I have organized my explanations of the typical provisions in a Purchase Agreement by using paragraph headings customarily found in a Purchase Agreement. Of course, different drafters might use slightly different headings, but the explanations will still apply.

These explanations are provided to help you better understand the Purchase Agreement. They are not intended to take the place of a lawyer's advice. If you have any questions or concerns about the provisions in your particular Purchase Agreement, you can use these explanations as a starting point, but I highly recommend you consult with your business lawyer for her input and further explanation of the particular provisions in your Purchase Agreement.

An Asset Purchase Agreement for a deal with a separate signing and closing typically contains the following terms and conditions:

The Parties

The first paragraph of the Purchase Agreement typically will not have a title or heading. It is an introductory paragraph that identifies the parties to the deal (e.g., buyer, seller, and, in some instances, individuals). It also contains the date of the Purchase Agreement. The biggest problem I usually see with the first paragraph is a failure to name the correct parties to the deal. For example, you may have set up a limited liability company to purchase the assets, but the Purchase Agreement identifies you, as an individual, as the buyer. Likewise, the assets of the business might be owned by a corporation, but the seller is identified in the opening paragraph as the individual who owns the corporation.

Sometimes, parties are missing from the opening paragraph. For example, if the Purchase Agreement contains provisions that should be binding on the owner of the selling corporation, then that individual needs to be named as a party to the Purchase Agreement for the contract to be binding on and enforceable against that individual. If the individual is not included as a party to the Purchase Agreement, he is not bound by the contract, and you have no promise from him.

Recitals or Purpose

Some Purchase Agreements contain a set of introductory paragraphs entitled, "Recitals." Recitals usually summarize the background leading up to the deal. Some argue that they are not enforceable unless the Purchase Agreement contains a provision indicating that they are. Recitals are not legally necessary. They are an old practice. If your Purchase Agreement contains Recitals, you should ensure that they reflect reality. You shouldn't need to spend much time or effort on the Recitals.

A more modern practice of drafting Purchase Agreements is to include a "Purpose" paragraph instead of Recitals. The Purpose paragraph will briefly describe the purpose and intent of the parties and will be an enforceable contract provision.

Purchased Assets

The Purchase Agreement needs to contain a clear and detailed description of the assets you are buying. Most Purchase Agreements contain a paragraph that lists general categories of certain assets (e.g., equipment, inventory, and contracts) and refers to exhibits or schedules attached to the Purchase Agreement that contain a detailed list of the assets in each category. Also, the Purchased Assets paragraph may list other assets, such as the telephone numbers of the business, the domain name, and intellectual property (trademarks, trade secrets, copyrights, and patents) being sold.

Avoid phrases, such as "all the assets of the business," and see that the Purchase Agreement contains a detailed list of the assets you are buying. A detailed list will avoid any disputes about what the seller is keeping, and what you are purchasing.

Excluded Assets

The seller usually keeps some assets, which are called "excluded assets." The Purchase Agreement customarily contains a paragraph that identifies which assets the seller will keep. For example, the seller customarily keeps cash on hand and accounts receivables. Those assets will be listed in the excluded assets paragraph. The paragraph will be similar to the Purchased Assets paragraph in that it will contain a general list of assets the seller will keep and refer to an exhibit or schedule that lists those assets with specificity. The exhibit listing excluded assets might include assets such as personal artwork and a laptop computer that the seller will keep.

If the Purchased Assets paragraph does not list a particular asset and the Excluded Assets paragraph doesn't list that particular asset, who owns it after closing? Probably the seller. You want the excluded assets paragraph and exhibit to be specific so that you won't be surprised when you walk into the business after closing. You don't want to find out that the seller has removed office furniture and computers from the business because those items didn't appear on a Purchased Assets or Excluded Assets list.

Purchase Price

The purchase price is the value you will give the seller in exchange for title to the assets you are buying. The purchase price is almost always money, but it could be other items. It might be a promise, such as your promise to pay off the seller's debt, or to employ the owner of the seller after the closing, or it could be another item, such as transfer of a vehicle you own in exchange for the assets you are buying. The purchase price also could be a combination of money, promises, and assets.

The purchase price also might include compensation for promises the seller's owner will make. For example, if you want to restrict the owner's ability to open a competing business after closing, you might offer to pay her a certain amount of money at or after closing in exchange for her written promise not to compete against the target or solicit the business's customers or employees for a period of time after closing.

In addition, the purchase price might include compensation for services the seller's owner will provide to your business after the closing. For example, you might enter into a consulting agreement with the owner for services to help you transition key customers, for training about how to operate the business, or for services the owner will provide directly to your business's customers until you can become proficient at providing those services, or hire an employee who is proficient in those services.

The purchase price (or at least a portion of it) might be calculated based on a formula. Sometimes the buyer and seller cannot agree on the purchase price because some of the assets to be sold are difficult to value. For example, if the seller has contracts or relationships with key customers, but cannot predict how much business those customers will bring to the business, the seller may believe the contracts have one value (e.g., based on past performance), but the buyer may believe the basis for assessing a value is too uncertain. As a result, the buyer and seller might agree to a formula for paying the seller additional money for a period after closing based on the revenues received under those contracts.

Likewise, if the buyer feels that the basis for valuing the entire business is uncertain, then she might negotiate a lower initial payment of the purchase price at closing, with increases to the purchase price based on the revenues of the entire business for a limited period of time after closing. This approach is often called an "earn out," and shifts some of the risks of post-closing success of the business to the seller-owner. An earn-out is a helpful tool for resolving an impasse about the amount of the purchase price. If the seller-owner will be involved with your business after closing, the earn out also gives her incentive to help your business become successful because the more success you experience, the higher her earn-out payments will be.

The purchase price might be adjusted at or shortly after closing. For example, if the target business, such as a retail store, has a lot of inventory, and that inventory fluctuates, a portion of the purchase price probably should be based on the amount of inventory on hand at closing. The exact value of the inventory cannot be determined without actually counting and pricing the inventory. Many times, the buyer and seller count inventory together at or very shortly after closing. The purchase price then is adjusted after closing to reflect the exact amount of the inventory on hand.

Make sure the purchase price paragraph clearly describes the purchase price. If a portion of the purchase price is based on an inventory count, the purchase price paragraph should indicate what values will be applied to the inventory once the count has been finished (e.g., the wholesale price originally paid by the seller, including any discounts or rebates). If a portion of the purchase price is to be based on post-closing revenues, the purchase price paragraph should explain the origin of the revenues (e.g., certain contracts or customers) and how revenues will be determined (e.g., excluding sales tax, net of buyer's expenses associated with performing the services, or net of any collection costs the buyer incurred to collect the revenues).

Payment Terms

The payment terms paragraph explains how you will pay the purchase price to the seller. In many small business deals, the buyer will pay the seller all of the money at closing. The Purchase Agreement probably will require that the money be paid in cash or immediately available funds, such as a certified check or wire transfer. The seller does not want to take the risk of transferring its assets to you and then waiting a day or two to see if your personal or business check will clear.

You should be aware that the requirement to bring immediately available funds to closing imposes two additional responsibilities. First, you will need to go to your bank before closing to arrange for a certified check or wire transfer. Second, you probably will have to pay your bank a small fee for the wire transfer or certified check. These responsibilities are minor logistics you will need to work out in preparation for closing.

If the seller requires you to pay a portion of the purchase price as a deposit when you sign the Purchase Agreement, then the Payment Terms paragraph should indicate the amount of the deposit, who will hold it until closing (e.g., the seller's attorney), and how you can get a refund of the deposit if you don't close the deal. It also should indicate that the deposit will be applied to the purchase price at closing. Typically, you can get a refund if you terminate the deal before the end of your due diligence period or if the seller breaches the Purchase Agreement or fails to close the deal.

If the seller is financing a portion of the purchase price by allowing you to pay some money at closing and then deliver a promissory note for the balance of the purchase price, the payment terms paragraph needs to explain clearly the terms of the seller financing. For example, the payment terms paragraph should identify the original principal amount of the promissory note, the interest rate, the time period (e.g., 12 months), how often payments will be made (e.g., monthly), when payments will be due (e.g., on the 1st day of each month), and whether the payments will be equal or not. If the promissory note will be interest-only or interest-free for a period, the payment terms paragraph should indicate the length of that time period. If the payments under the promissory note will be amortized using a period that is different from the number of payments (e.g., a 60-month payment period amortized over 120 months), the payment terms paragraph needs to explain that. Ultimately, the purchase terms paragraph needs to include a clear description of the essential terms of the promissory note to avoid a later dispute.

Sometimes, part of the purchase price will be held in escrow for a limited period of time after closing. For example, if the purchase price was calculated in part based on an estimated value of inventory, you might insist that a portion of the purchase price be held in escrow until the actual value of the inventory on hand is determined. If the actual value is less than the initial estimated value, the difference will be refunded to you out of the escrow funds. This protects you from the risk of the seller not having the funds when you request the refund.

An escrow of a portion of the purchase price also might be used if you believe it is likely you might be asked to pay for certain items that are the seller's responsibility, such as refunds for pre-closing purchases. In addition, you might require an escrow if you are worried the seller might not be able to satisfy its indemnity responsibilities (see below). An escrow for this purpose gives you a pool of money from which to draw if you make a claim against the seller.

Allocation of Purchase Price

Both the seller and the buyer will be required to report the asset sale to the IRS and the appropriate state taxing authority. Both parties want to ensure that their respective tax returns match to avoid a review of the deal by the taxing authority. In addition, the parties want to allocate the purchase price to minimize taxes, if possible, without being so unreasonable as to trigger an audit by the taxing authority.

The purchase price is based on an aggregation of the values of the assets being purchased. The seller will experience different tax consequences for different types of assets being sold. For example, the portion of the purchase price allocated to the seller's non-competition promise might be taxed to the seller as ordinary income, while the portion of the purchase price allocated to the value of equipment sold might be taxed to the seller as capital gains. Ordinary income and capital gains may be taxed at different rates, with one being lower than the other. As a result, the seller might want to try to allocate as much of the purchase price to the asset category with a lower tax rate (typically capital gains), if possible. The buyer also is interested in the allocation of the purchase price because it will affect its tax basis in the assets, which may impact the buyer's taxes at a later date, such as when the Buyer subsequently sells the business.

The Purchase Agreement may contain a paragraph that requires the buyer and seller to agree upon the purchase price allocation at closing. The allocation might appear in a separate document the parties will sign at closing, or the parties might also fill out and agree upon the contents of an IRS Form 8594 at closing. More often, I see Purchase Agreements that simply require the buyer and seller to agree upon the purchase price allocation after closing. You need to be careful with that type of provision because it might be an unenforceable "agreement to agree" (see Chapter 10). Another approach I see in Purchase Agreements is a paragraph that allows the seller to determine the allocation, requires the buyer to adopt that allocation, and prohibits the buyer from challenging the allocation or reporting a different allocation.

In small business deals, purchase price allocation might not be a significant issue because the dollars involved and the corresponding potential tax consequences may not be great. In these deals, the buyer and seller typically adopt the seller's reasonable valuation of the tangible assets being sold (e.g., based on the depreciated value of those assets appearing in the seller's financial records). Then they subtract that amount from the total purchase price. If the purchase price includes compensation for non-competition promises, then that compensation is allocated accordingly. The parties then allocate the remainder of the purchase price to the goodwill of the business.

Due Diligence or Inspection Period; Right to Terminate

The Purchase Agreement should contain a paragraph that gives you a limited period of time to inspect the target business and its assets and to terminate the deal if you discover something you don't like. No less than 30 days for a due diligence period is customary and reasonable unless the time needs to be shorter because the closing will happen less than 30 days from the date on which you sign the Purchase Agreement. A due diligence period beyond 90 days probably is unreasonable. 60 days is a good compromise, if possible.

If you think you will need more time than 30 days for your due diligence, then you might consider asking for language in the Purchase Agreement that gives you the option to extend an initial 30-day due diligence period for another 30 days, if you pay more money into the deposit. For example, if the initial deposit was $10,000, the option to extend the due diligence period might require you to pay in an additional $10,000 as an additional deposit in exchange for the extension. The $20,000 of total deposit would be applied to the purchase price at closing. In a few instances, I have seen a seller require that the additional deposit is non-refundable if you decide to terminate the deal, but I suggest avoiding that requirement, if possible.

The due diligence paragraph should give you broad rights to inspect every aspect of the target business, including financial records, customer lists, vendor and supplier lists, accounting software, equipment, contracts, environmental issues, and real property. You might also ask for the right to interview key employees. This is a delicate request because the seller might not want her employees to know about the impending sale. At the least, you should have the right to ask the seller's owner about the target business and any information you are reviewing. You probably will be asked to promise that all this information be kept confidential and that you will not use it for your own purposes or disclose it if you decide to terminate the deal. That's reasonable.

The due diligence paragraph probably will restrict the times you can conduct your due diligence, such as during the regular business hours of the target business. It might also require you to provide some prior notice (such as a day or two) before you come to the target business for your inspection. Those restrictions are customary and reasonable. Any restriction on the number of times you can come to the target business for inspection, however, is unreasonable.

The due diligence paragraph probably also will require you to promise that you will indemnify (i.e., pay or reimburse) the seller for any losses or damages it suffers as a result of your investigation. For example, if you crash a vehicle while taking it for a test drive, you will be required to pay or reimburse the seller for the repairs. This promise is customary and reasonable.

The due diligence paragraph also should explain how you are to notify the seller if you want to terminate the deal based on your due diligence findings. Usually, you will be required to deliver written notice of termination to the seller before the expiration of the due diligence period. The due diligence paragraph should not limit the reasons for which you can terminate the deal. Instead, the termination decision should be in your sole and absolute discretion. As a result, you should not be required to identify or explain the basis for your termination, and any contractual requirement to do so would not be reasonable or customary.

Financing Contingency

If you need to get a loan to finance part or all of the purchase price, then you need to put a paragraph in the Purchase Agreement that allows you to get out of the deal if you are unable to obtain a loan. This is a customary and reasonable paragraph, but it also is customary that the financing contingency has some reasonable limitations. A financing contingency without reasonable limitations would be unfair to the seller.

Reasonable limitations on the financing contingency include setting a period of time you will have to obtain the loan or terminate the deal. For example, you might be required to obtain the loan by the end of the due diligence period. You also might consider putting a limitation in the financing contingency about your ability to choose your lender, in your sole discretion, and the minimum dollar amount of the loan sought. You could also place limitations on the maximum interest rate and term of the loan sought, but those limitations really are not necessary because you should see that the paragraph gives you the sole discretion to accept or reject the loan. In other words, there should not be any language in the financing contingency paragraph that requires you to enter into a loan that meets certain minimum standards.

A buyer usually satisfies the financing contingency by entering into a written, binding loan commitment with its lender. If the buyer does not believe it will enter into a binding loan commitment before the end of the financing contingency period, then it will need to decide whether to terminate the deal or take the risk of moving forward under the uncertainty of not having financing in place.

Assignment and Assumption of Contracts

If certain licenses, equipment leases, creditor, customer, vendor, or supplier contracts are being purchased as part of the assets of the target business, then the Purchase Agreement should contain a paragraph by which the seller agrees to transfer (i.e., assign) those contracts to the buyer, and the buyer agrees to assume responsibility for them beginning on the closing date.

If the seller paid a security deposit on any contract to be transferred to the buyer, this paragraph should indicate what will happen to that deposit. For example, the Purchase Agreement might require the buyer to pay a new, substitute deposit and allow the seller to obtain a refund of its deposit or the Purchase Agreement might indicate that the security deposit will be transferred to the buyer, with the buyer reimbursing the seller for that deposit as an additional expense at closing. The latter approach is more customary and easier to administer.

If any of those contracts requires the licensor's, equipment lessor's, creditor's, customer's, vendor's, or supplier's consent before it can be assigned, this paragraph should indicate that the transfer of those contracts is contingent on obtaining that consent before closing. If the assignment and assumption of contracts are critical to the deal, this paragraph should make closing contingent on the successful assignment and assumption of the contracts. In other words, the deal will not close, and each party will walk away without any liability to the other party if the contracts are not or cannot be assigned. In that case, the buyer also would receive a refund of its deposit.

Assignment and Assumption of Lease or New Lease

If the target business is located in leased space, the buyer will need to either assume the existing lease or enter into a new lease to be able to remain in that space after closing. The Purchase Agreement should have a paragraph addressing this. I draft Purchase Agreements for my buyers to give my buyers the option to choose how to proceed. Entering into a new lease is less risky for a buyer than assuming a lease, because, under a new lease, the buyer will not be responsible for the seller's potential liabilities under the old lease.

If the lease is going to be assigned to the buyer, you should review the lease to determine whether the landlord's consent is required before the assignment can be valid. Most leases require the landlord's consent. Some leases contain detailed requirements for obtaining that consent and impose an administrative or legal fee to be paid to the landlord before the consent will be given. The assignment and assumption paragraph in the Purchase Agreement should indicate who will pay that fee.

The seller probably paid a security deposit when it signed the lease. If the lease is being assigned to and assumed by the buyer, then this paragraph should indicate what will happen to that deposit. For example, the Purchase Agreement might require the buyer to pay a new, substitute deposit and allow the seller to obtain a refund of its deposit or the Purchase Agreement might indicate that the security deposit will be transferred to the buyer, with the buyer reimbursing the seller for that deposit as an additional expense at closing. The latter approach is more customary and easier to administer.

Regardless of whether the buyer will be assuming the existing lease or entering into a new lease at closing, the paragraph about the lease should make the deal contingent on the successful lease assignment or entry into a new lease. The buyer should have the right, in its sole discretion, to choose which option to pursue (subject to the landlord's requirements), and the right to reject the assignment and assumption or the new lease if the buyer cannot get acceptable terms from the landlord. If the buyer is not satisfied with the proposed terms of the assignment and assumption or new lease, the buyer should be able to terminate the deal. In that case, the deal will not close, and each party will walk away without any liability to the other party if the contracts are not or cannot be assigned. The buyer also would receive a refund of its deposit.

No Assumption (or Limited Assumption) of Seller's Liabilities

One of the buyer's biggest reasons for purchasing the target business's assets is to avoid becoming responsible for the seller's liabilities connected to its operation of the target business before closing. The Purchase Agreement should contain a paragraph that clearly states that the buyer is not assuming any of the seller's liabilities. This paragraph should require the seller to acknowledge that it will remain responsible for its liabilities. Of course, if the buyer is purchasing certain contracts or a lease as part of the assets, then this paragraph should recognize and acknowledge that the buyer is assuming the liabilities associated with those contracts arising after closing. Even in this instance, however, this paragraph should clearly indicate that the buyer will not be responsible, and the seller will remain responsible, for all liabilities associated with those contracts arising out of events occurring before closing.

Prorations

The target business probably will have operating expenses that are paid before closing for items or services that will be provided after closing. Common examples of these types of expenses include rent, utilities, and taxes. For example, if the seller pays rent on May 1st, and closing occurs on May 15th, then the buyer should be required to reimburse the seller for 17 days of rent at closing because the seller owned the business for only the first 14 days of the month. Likewise, if the seller paid personal property taxes on business equipment for the second half of the year, but only owns the equipment for three of six months, the buyer should reimburse the seller for one-half of those taxes at closing.

If items are paid in arrears—i.e., the services are performed for a period that straddles the time period before and after closing, but fees for those services are not invoiced until after closing, then the Purchase Agreement should allow the buyer to seek the seller's payment of its portion of those fees for the pre-closing period. If those amounts are known at closing, then they can be offset against the purchase price as a credit to the buyer.

The Purchase Agreement usually has a paragraph, or at least a sentence, indicating that prepaid expenses will be prorated among the buyer and seller at closing or within a short time period after closing. Such a paragraph is necessary, customary, and reasonable.

Prepaids, Customer Deposits

Depending on what the target business does, the seller may have taken advance payments (i.e., "prepaids") or deposits from its customers for services to be performed or goods to be sold after closing. For example, I represented the owner of franchise store who was purchasing an additional store from another franchisee. When a customer orders something from that store, they pay for it by credit card before the order is filled. The order may be filled several days after the order has been placed. As a result, the seller and buyer knew that the seller might receive orders and take payments several days before the closing for items that would not be delivered until after closing. The Purchase Agreement needed a paragraph indicating that the seller would transfer that prepaid money to the buyer.

Likewise, if customers are required to make a down payment or deposit for services or goods, the Purchase Agreement should indicate how those down payments or deposits will be transferred. It would be unfair for the seller to keep that money.

In the event the seller performs some of the services or delivers some of the goods before closing, and the buyer performs or delivers the rest after closing, this paragraph also should indicate that the prepaids or deposits will be allocated among the seller and the buyer in accordance with each party's respective contribution.

If you fail to include a paragraph in the Purchase Agreement about how the prepaids and customer deposits will be handled, then the seller will get to keep that money, and you might find yourself in a position after closing where you are performing services or delivering goods and not getting paid for them.

Post-Closing Transition

If you want the seller's owner to train you, introduce you to customers, be on call for questions, or help in any other way with the transition of the business, then make sure the Purchase Agreement has language in it about those services. Do not have a paragraph that simply says something along the lines of "owner will assist the buyer with the transition of the business." Instead, be clear and specific about the types of services the owner will perform, the hours during which services will be performed (e.g., regular business hours), how the owner will perform (e.g., onsite, at customer locations, by phone, by email, or a combination of these), and the time period during which the owner will be obligated to perform (e.g., for 90 days after closing).

The seller's owner likely will want to be paid for his services. Whether to pay additional compensation for transition services depends on the nature and amount of services to be provided. If the transition services will be minimal, such as being on call by phone or email to answer questions about routine operating procedures, then you probably do not need to pay additional compensation. In that case, you should make sure the post-closing services paragraph contains language requiring the seller to acknowledge that compensation for those services is covered by the purchase price.

If the owner's post-closing services will be more extensive, then it is fair to compensate the owner. Compensation usually is paid on an agreed upon hourly rate, but you could be more creative if you like. For example, you might offer discounts on products, payment of health insurance premiums, payment of professional organization fees for a limited time period, or payment of health club or country club membership dues for a limited period. You also should reimburse the owner for reasonable business expenses incurred in the performance of his services, such as travel and lodging, in accordance with your company's reimbursement policy. The Purchase Agreement language about compensation and reimbursement should be clear and specific, including how compensation will be measured, when it will be paid, and any deductions you will withhold.

If the post-closing transition services are minimal, then a paragraph in the Purchase Agreement probably will be adequate to handle the issue. If the owner will be acting in a consultant role, then you probably want the owner to sign a separate, written consulting agreement with your new business that spells out the terms and conditions of the relationship in clear detail. In that case, the consulting agreement should be attached as an exhibit to the Purchase Agreement, and the Purchase Agreement should obligate the owner to enter into the consulting agreement at closing.

Representations and Warranties

The Purchase Agreement should contain some representations and warranties. Representations are written statements of significant facts that a party agrees to in the contract. Warranties are promises one party makes to the other party in the contract. Representations and warranties relate to each party's ability to enter into the deal and to the operation of the target business. The seller typically makes the bulk of the representations and warranties.

Representations and Warranties Made by Both Parties
There are typically four types of representations and warranties that each party to the Purchase Agreement will make to the other. They relate to entity organization, authority to sign the contract, the absence of any conflicts with other agreements, and the absence or recognition of brokers.

(1) <u>Due Organization</u>: In this paragraph, a party will represent and promise that its entity (e.g., corporation or limited liability company) has been properly formed and is in good standing. The reason for this paragraph is to avoid the risk of making a contract with an entity that does not exist, which would void the deal. This paragraph is necessary, but typically does not need negotiation, unless the facts and circumstances need to be properly reflected in the paragraph.

(2) <u>Due Execution</u>: In this paragraph, a party will represent and promise that the party can enter into the deal and that the Purchase Agreement was signed by someone who has the authority to bind the party to the contract. The reason for this paragraph is to avoid the risk of having an unenforceable contract because the person signing didn't have the authority to make a binding contract. This paragraph is necessary but typically does not need negotiation.

(3) <u>No Conflicts</u>: Each party will represent and promise to the other party that entering into the Purchase Agreement will not conflict with or breach any other contract. The reason for this paragraph is to avoid the risk of entering into

the Purchase Agreement and then finding out that someone else can stop your deal. For example, if the seller has entered into a letter of intent that contains a paragraph granting another potential buyer the exclusive right for six months to purchase the target business's assets, and then enters into a Purchase Agreement with you during the third month, the other potential buyer will be able to stop your deal and buy the assets, even after you have invested a lot of time and money in conducting your due diligence and negotiating the Purchase Agreement. This paragraph is necessary, but typically does not require any negotiation, unless the facts and circumstances need to be properly reflected in the paragraph.

(4) <u>Brokers</u>: Each party will represent and promise to the other party that no brokers have been involved in the deal. Or, if a broker has been involved, this paragraph will identify the broker and represent and promise that no other brokers have been involved in the deal. Sometimes, this paragraph also may indicate which party is responsible for paying the broker's commission, or that issue might be handled later in a separate paragraph in the Purchase Agreement. The reason for this paragraph is to avoid the risk of having a broker surface to claim a portion of the purchase price as a commission. This paragraph is necessary, but typically does not require any negotiation, unless the facts and circumstances need to be properly reflected in the paragraph.

Representations and Warranties Made by the Seller

The seller should make certain representations and promises about the nature of the target business and its assets and operations. At a minimum, a buyer should require that the seller make the following representations and warranties:

(1) <u>Title to Assets</u>: The seller should represent and promise that it has good and marketable title to the assets being sold. This paragraph should clearly state that there are no liens against the assets. If liens exist, however, the seller should identify those liens in writing in the Purchase Agreement. Typically, this disclosure is accomplished by attaching an exhibit to the Purchase Agreement listing the liens. If liens exist, this paragraph should require that the seller pays them off at closing, out of the purchase price proceeds, so that the buyer gets title to the assets without any liens. This paragraph is necessary to avoid the risk of the buyer buying assets that have liens against them. Leaving liens on purchased assets will give the seller's creditors the ability to foreclose on the assets to satisfy the seller's debts, even after closing. In that instance, you would lose the assets, even though you paid for them. This paragraph goes to the essence of the buyer's ownership of the purchased assets.

(2) <u>Condition of Assets</u>: In this paragraph, the seller represents and promises that the purchased assets are in good working condition. This avoids the risk of buying an asset that does not work, which would require you to pay to replace or repair that asset after closing. In many instances, the seller might be selling the assets "AS IS," and, therefore, refuse to provide a warranty about the condition of the assets. That might be reasonable, especially if you have the right to inspect the assets before closing and to call off the deal if you find a problem.

(3) <u>No Claims</u>: The seller should represent and promise that no one has filed or threatened to file a lawsuit against the seller or the target business, that no government agency is investigating, threatening to investigate or has filed or threatened to file a claim against the seller or target

business, and that no judgments or court orders have been entered against the seller or target business. The reason for this paragraph is to avoid the risk of someone filing a lien (called a "judgment lien") against the purchased assets to satisfy a judgment received in connection with a lawsuit or governmental claim. This paragraph is necessary and negotiable only to the extent it needs to reflect the facts and circumstances of the target business.

(4) <u>No Breach of Contracts and Leases</u>: This is another paragraph designed to avoid the risk that someone might stop your deal because they have a claim against the seller or the purchased assets. The seller should represent and promise that its contracts and leases are in full force, and that neither the seller nor any other party to any contract or lease has defaulted. The buyer wants this paragraph to avoid a potential post-closing claim against it for the seller's breach. In addition, the buyer does not want to purchase a contract or lease that has been breached by the other party because the buyer does not want to take on the time and expense of enforcing a contract shortly after closing.

(5) <u>Taxes</u>: Many sellers have problems with taxes. I have handled many deals in which the seller was selling, in large part, to get money to pay off large tax bills that were long overdue. This is a common risk with businesses that have many employees or businesses that are required to pay sales tax, such as restaurants. In those types of businesses, taxes accumulate quickly, and business owners might get into a pattern of deferring payment until their cash flow improves. Tax agencies can collect back taxes by filing a lien against the target business's assets. The tax agency can then foreclose upon and sell those assets to collect on back taxes, interest, and civil penalties. If you purchase assets on

which tax liens have been recorded or could be recorded, you might risk losing those assets in foreclosure. As a result, the buyer wants the seller to represent and promise that all taxes, including income, property, payroll, and sales taxes, have been paid before or will be paid at closing out of the purchase price proceeds.

(6) <u>Compliance with Law</u>: The Seller should represent and promise that it has operated the target business in compliance with applicable laws and regulations. This representation and warranty is designed to avoid the risk of the buyer purchasing assets that might be subject to a lawsuit or government agency investigation or action. Depending on the nature of the target business, you might want to reference by name specific laws you believe might present a significant risk, such as specific environmental laws.

(7) <u>Complete and True Information</u>: The Buyer wants to make sure it has received all of the information about the operation of the business, including financial information, tax history, employee records, vendor and customer information, and contracts. Include in the Purchase Agreement a paragraph in which the seller represents and promises that it has provided all the information about the target business and that the information is true. The buyer needs this promise to avoid the risk of basing its decision to purchase on incomplete, inaccurate, or false information, which might result in the buyer taking on more risk than it anticipated.

(8) <u>Employees</u>: You are not obligated to hire the seller's employees unless you agree to do so in the Purchase Agreement. Even if you don't hire the employees, you might become responsible for claims employees make against the target

business after closing for things that happened before closing. Therefore, the seller should represent and promise that it has paid or will pay all wages and salaries, that it has paid or will pay all payroll taxes, and that it does not have any profit-sharing or retirement plans for its employees.

(9) <u>AS IS Disclaimer</u>: Most small business asset sales are made on an "AS IS" basis. In a true AS IS deal, the seller makes no promises about the assets or the target business's operations. In that instance, you get the assets and the business in whatever condition they are in. Even though the seller might argue that this is fair because you have an inspection right, I suggest not agreeing to a true AS IS deal because you probably don't have the time, expertise, or desire to spend the money to hire someone to evaluate every aspect of the target business. Instead, obtaining the representations and warranties from the seller described above, and allowing the seller to disclaim all other express and implied representations and warranties is more customary and reasonable.

<u>Knowledge Qualifiers</u>: This is not a representation or warranty, but an approach by which a seller might try to limit or qualify its representations and promises. For example, the seller might ask to insert language into the Compliance with Laws paragraph to indicate that she is making the promise based only on her "actual knowledge." The seller asks for these qualifications to avoid the risk of being held liable for breaching a promise when something is discovered that was out of her control. For example, if a prior owner of the target business spilled hazardous materials at the business site, the seller might not know about that incident and should not be in breach of the Purchase Agreement after the incident is discovered. Knowledge qualifiers are

reasonable in some instances for certain representations and warranties, but not others. In addition, allowing the seller to insert a knowledge qualifier into some representations and warranties might be acceptable if reasonable due diligence has satisfied you that the representation and warranty at issue probably is true. Your business lawyer will help you determine which knowledge qualifiers are reasonable.

Representations and Warranties Made by the Buyer
The seller will want the buyer to make certain representations and warranties to the seller in the Purchase Agreement. Most of those representations and warranties are discussed above in the section about representations and warranties made by both parties.

The only other representation and warranty the seller might request from the buyer is a representation and warranty about the buyer's due diligence. The seller wants to avoid the risk of the buyer claiming it has been damaged by something the buyer learned after closing. When I represent a seller in an asset sale, I include a paragraph in the Purchase Agreement that requires the buyer to make the following representations and promises about its due diligence:

- She has had the opportunity to visit with the seller to discuss the target business;
- All materials and information requested by the buyer have been provided to the buyer to the buyer's reasonable satisfaction;
- The buyer has made its own independent examination, investigation, analysis, and evaluation of the purchased assets and the target business, including the buyer's own estimate of the value of the purchased assets and the target business;

- The buyer has undertaken the due diligence (including a review of the assets, liabilities, books, records, and contracts of the seller) the buyer deems adequate;
- If the buyer is an employee of the target business, a representation and warranty that the buyer has intimate knowledge of the target business because the buyer has been an employee of the seller; and
- If the buyer has experience in the target business's industry, a representation and warranty to that effect.

It is reasonable for a buyer to make these representations and warranties, as long as they reflect the reality of the facts and circumstances. Your business lawyer can help you determine whether the actual language of these representations and warranties is reasonable.

Pre-Closing Obligations

The buyer wants to prevent the seller from slacking off during the period after the Purchase Agreement has been signed and before closing. The buyer should ensure the Purchase Agreement contains a paragraph that requires the seller to do the following before closing:

- operate the target business as the seller always has;
- maintain the target business's relationships with customers, suppliers, vendors, and contractors; and
- maintain inventory at ordinary levels so the buyer has the inventory it needs to operate the business when it takes over after closing.
- not enter into any significant contracts, without telling you and getting your written consent first.

Closing Date

The Purchase Agreement should identify a specific closing date. This is the date title to the assets will be transferred from the seller to the buyer. Some Purchase Agreements also indicate a time of day of the closing date on which title will transfer (e.g., 5:00 p.m. or close of business). If no time is indicated, title customarily transfers at 12:00 a.m. on the closing date, even if the closing is conducted later that day. In other words, the buyer becomes responsible for the business on the closing date.

Employees

You are under no obligation to hire any of the seller's employees. Likewise, the seller is under no obligation to guarantee that its employees will accept employment from you after closing. If, however, you desire to employ certain employees after closing, you will want a paragraph in which the seller acknowledges that you can employ them. Of course, you cannot force any person to be employed, but you can ask the seller to assist you with the recruitment of the seller's employees.

Taxes

The seller probably will want a paragraph in the Purchase Agreement that requires the buyer to pay any sales or transfer taxes associated with transferring title to the assets. For example, if the assets include vehicles, the seller will want the buyer to pay fees related to transferring vehicle titles and obtaining new registrations. That is customary.

Conditions Precedent

The Purchase Agreement likely will contain a section that lists a number of conditions that must be satisfied before a party will be required to close the deal. For example, if consents are required to transfer a lease or other contract, the buyer will not be required to close until those consents are obtained. The buyer will also not be required to close if there have been any adverse changes to the business during the period between signing the Purchase Agreement and closing. In addition, each party will require that all of the representations and warranties made by the other party are still true at the time of closing. The conditions precedent paragraph should list the documents that must be signed and delivered by each party before or at closing. Of course, the seller will want to require that the buyer pay the purchase price at closing, which is reasonable.

Personal Liability for Entity Obligations

If the target business is owned by an entity, you risk a post-closing scenario where you make a claim against the seller entity (e.g., for payment of a loss from something the seller did before closing), but the seller entity has no money because it has paid out all of the purchase price proceeds to business creditors and the entity owners. To avoid that risk, you should ask the individual owners of the seller to personally guarantee the selling entity's obligations under the Purchase Agreement. If the selling entity has more than one shareholder or member, you should ask all the owners to provide personal guaranties. These personal guaranties might not mean much if an owner can put personal assets out of reach by titling them in his or her spouse's name. Therefore, if a selling entity's owner agrees to give you a personal guaranty, you also should get their spouse to join in the guaranty. The Purchase Agreement should have a paragraph setting out these requirements, which also requires those giving personal guaranties to sign and deliver a separate document at closing containing the guaranty.

If there is more than one personal guarantor, then each individual's personal guaranty should be "joint and several." This means that each guarantor will be personally responsible for all of the debt. It allows you to pursue whichever personal guarantor you believe can pay the debt, without any obligation on you to try to apportion among and collect a portion of the debt from each personal guarantor.

If you ask the owners of the seller entity to provide personal guaranties, be prepared for them to ask you (and your spouse) to personally guarantee the obligations of your buyer entity. That reciprocal request is reasonable, and you should be willing to give it because getting the seller owner's personal guaranty is probably more valuable to you than your guaranty will be to the seller.

Note that if the Purchase Agreement contains language intended to bind the individual owners of an entity, those individual owners also should be parties to and sign the Purchase Agreement, even if only for the limited purpose of binding them to certain provisions of the Purchase Agreement.

Non-Competition Restriction

If you are concerned that a seller will start a competing business or go to work for a competitor after closing, you will want the Purchase Agreement to contain a paragraph that prohibits the seller from doing so. Drafting non-competition restrictions is tricky and should be handled only by a business lawyer who is familiar with the case law about what constitutes an enforceable non-competition agreement in your state.

In Virginia, non-competition restrictions are enforceable only if (1) the geographic area in which the person is prohibited from competing is reasonable, (2) the scope of services the seller is prohibited from performing is reasonable, and (3) the length of time of the non-competition restriction is reasonable. Virginia courts are more likely to enforce a non-competition restriction associated with an asset sale, than in an employment agreement, but you still need to be careful about how the non-competition restrictions are drafted. In Virginia, many non-competes are judged unenforceable because the scope of services restriction is not properly drafted.

Asking for a non-competition restriction in the Purchase Agreement is reasonable, but negotiating its scope and limitations also is customary and reasonable.

Non-Solicitation Restriction

If you are concerned that the seller will take your customers or employees after closing, then you will want the Purchase Agreement to contain a paragraph that prohibits the seller from doing so. In some instances, I have seen Purchase Agreements with non-solicitation restrictions that also prevent a seller from working with or ordering from certain vendors, suppliers, and independent contractors after closing.

It is customary to pair a non-competition paragraph with a non-solicitation paragraph because both types of restrictions work hand-in-hand to protect you from any seller attempt to profit from the sale of the target business and then stripping the value of the target business by starting a competing business and taking your customers and employees.

Drafting non-solicitation restrictions can be risky because they won't be enforceable if improperly or unreasonably drafted. One potential drafting trap is a poorly drafted definition of which customers cannot be solicited. Your business lawyer can help you with that. The non-solicitation period usually will be identical in length to the non-competition period.

Confidentiality; No Press Releases

The Purchase Agreement should contain confidentiality restrictions that protect both parties. You want the seller to keep all of the information about the deal confidential, including the purchase price and the terms and conditions of the Purchase Agreement. You do not want customers, vendors, suppliers, or employees to leave the target business before closing because they discover the deal and get nervous. You'll want a reasonable opportunity shortly after closing to convince them to stay.

The seller also wants to keep that information confidential for many of the same reasons. The seller does not want to lose business, customers, vendors, suppliers, or employees before closing. Before closing, the risk always exists that the deal will not close, either because the buyer terminates the deal during the due diligence period, or the conditions precedent cannot be satisfied. In the event the deal does not close, the seller wants to make sure the target business still has value so the seller can either continue to operate the business or put the business back on the market for sale.

The Purchase Agreement typically contains a prohibition against any press releases before closing announcing the sale of or that the business will be under new management. That prohibition is reasonable.

Bulk Sales

Some states have laws that require notice to creditors and the local taxing authorities before a business can sell its inventory or all of its assets. These laws are typically called, "Bulk Sales Acts." Bulk Sales Acts may require the payment of taxes on the transfer of the inventory or assets. The purpose of the Bulk Sales Acts is to protect the seller's creditors from losing the ability to come after the seller's assets to collect on debts.

Bulk Sales Acts can add additional work and costs to a deal because the Acts have procedures for providing notice to creditors prior to the sale, and providing a list of creditors and schedule of assets to the buyer. The buyer is typically responsible for assuring that creditors are paid out of closing proceeds.

Often buyers and sellers choose not to notify creditors ahead of the sale so as to not slow down the deal or impact the target business's operations. The Purchase Agreement usually contains a paragraph by which the buyer and seller agree to waive compliance with the Bulk Sale Act, and this is a reasonable approach.

There is a significant risk to the buyer, however, because if the Bulk Sale Act is not complied with and the seller's creditor is not paid at closing out of the purchase price proceeds, the creditor may be able to disregard the sale and pursue the collection of the debt owed to it against the assets transferred to the buyer.

Indemnification

An indemnification provision is vital to allocate risk fairly between a seller and buyer. At the very least, the Purchase Agreement must contain a paragraph that requires the seller to indemnify the buyer for certain things.

An indemnification is a promise by one party to pay or reimburse the other party for losses, damages, costs, and expenses (e.g., reasonable attorney's fees) the other party experiences as a result of the first party's acts or omissions. It is critical that your Purchase Agreement contains an indemnification from the seller, and the seller likely will require that you indemnify it, too, which is reasonable.

The seller should indemnify the buyer for any losses, damages, costs, or expenses the buyer suffers after closing as a result of the seller's operation of the target business before closing or the seller's breach of the Purchase Agreement.

The buyer should indemnify the seller for any losses, damages, costs, or expenses the seller suffers after closing as a result of the buyer's operation of its business on and after closing or the buyer's breach of the Purchase Agreement.

Some Purchase Agreements also contain detailed paragraphs about how one party can make a claim for indemnification against another party and limitations on the amount to be paid. For example, some indemnification provisions contain a "deductible"—i.e., a limitation that will not require one party to indemnify the other party unless the amount claimed is over a certain dollar amount. In that instance, the indemnification covers only the amount in excess of the deductible.

An indemnification provision might contain a "basket." Imagine a fictional basket into which dollars are deposited. Losses, damages, costs, and expenses subject to indemnification are put in the basket, but paid out only after a certain dollar threshold is reached—i.e., when the basket is full—after which all losses, damages, costs, and expenses are paid from the first dollar (a "tipping basket"), unless a deductible also applies.

In addition, an indemnification provision also could contain a "cap." In that instance, the party would be required to indemnify the other party only up to a certain dollar limit, such as the amount of the purchase price.

Finally, an indemnification provision might also require the seller to put some of the purchase price into escrow for a limited period of time after closing to ensure that the buyer will have a source of funds if it makes a claim for indemnification.

Rarely do I see indemnification provisions containing these limitations in Purchase Agreements for small businesses, however.

Indemnification provisions also should contain an obligation for each party to defend the other party against claims made by third parties. For example, if a customer of the target business sues the buyer after closing for something the seller did before closing, the Purchase Agreement should require the seller to be responsible for the cost and expense of defending the buyer against that claim. The indemnification provision should give you a say in which lawyer is used and the right to approve any proposed settlement.

Many buyers and sellers avoid lengthy and detailed indemnification provisions because they don't understand their importance in allocating risks fairly between the parties. But indemnification provisions are critical, especially to the buyer, to ensure you won't have to pay for losses, damages, costs, and expenses caused by the seller. Your business lawyer should see that the indemnification adequately protects you, and you should not be terribly concerned about the amount of verbiage it adds to the Purchase Agreement.

Brokers
The Purchase Agreement should contain a provision by which the parties agree that no brokers were used in connection with the deal. Or, if brokers were used, the Purchase Agreement should contain a provision identifying the broker, quantifying the broker's

commission, and indicating who will be responsible for paying the broker. Without such a provision, you risk a situation where a broker emerges demanding payment of a commission. In that event, you want to be able to look to the Purchase Agreement to determine how to resolve that problem.

Boilerplate

The end of the Purchase Agreement will contain a section entitled, "Miscellaneous Provisions" or "General Provisions." The paragraphs in this section are commonly referred to as "boilerplate." You can research why it's called boilerplate, but you don't need to know why for purposes of buying a business. Some hold the position that these paragraphs are called "boilerplate" because they cannot be negotiated; others hold the position that the boilerplate paragraphs do not really impact the deal. Neither are true, as I'll explain below.

Paragraphs commonly found in the boilerplate section of a Purchase Agreement include:

(1) <u>Fees and Costs</u>: This paragraph should indicate that each party will be responsible for all of the fees and costs it incurs in connection with the deal, including professional fees (e.g., accountants and lawyers). If there is an attorney's fee shifting provision in the Purchase Agreement for disputes, you should ensure that the Fees and Costs paragraph refers to that provision as an exception for a party's responsibility for its fees and costs. The Fees and Costs paragraph may be negotiable if one party has agreed to pay part or all of another party's costs. For example, sometimes a seller will agree to pay a portion of the buyer's legal fees in connection with the deal as an incentive to the buyer.

(2) <u>Severability</u>: Contract law in your jurisdiction may dictate that if one part of the Purchase Agreement is unenforceable, the entire contract is void. The severability paragraph is included to avoid that risk. It provides that if any portion of the Purchase Agreement is unenforceable, then the remainder of the Purchase Agreement will still be enforceable and interpreted as if the unenforceable portion were no longer contained in the Purchase Agreement. This paragraph is necessary but typically requires no negotiation.

(3) <u>Entire Agreement or Merger</u>: Neither party wants to risk having the other party claim that the Purchase Agreement does not contain all the agreements they made about the purchase of the target business. To prevent that risk, the Purchase Agreement should contain a paragraph indicating that the Purchase Agreement contains all of the agreements made about the deal. That paragraph will indicate that the Purchase Agreement supersedes all prior negotiations, offers, verbal representations and warranties, and verbal and written communications that might be construed as agreements (e.g., emails). Lawyers refer to this contract principle as a "merger" of all prior communications into the Purchase Agreement. This paragraph is necessary but should reflect the reality of the circumstances. For example, if there are other agreements related to the deal, such as a separate written and signed Confidentiality Agreement between the buyer and seller, this paragraph should be changed to refer to that separate agreement and indicate that the Purchase Agreement does not invalidate it.

(4) <u>Modification or Amendment</u>: Neither party wants to take the risk that the other party might claim the Purchase Agreement has been amended without its permission.

For example, you do not want to risk the seller claiming that the purchase price was increased because you sent an email to the seller after signing the Purchase Agreement indicating that the value of the target business was higher than the purchase price. This paragraph allows for amendments or modifications to the Purchase Agreement, but only if those changes are in writing and signed by both parties. This paragraph is necessary, but usually does not require any negotiation, as long as it prevents either party from unilaterally changing the Purchase Agreement.

(5) <u>Waiver</u>: Neither party wants to take the risk that the other party might claim that it is no longer obligated to do something required by the Purchase Agreement because the first party did not enforce a breach. For example, if the Purchase Agreement requires the seller to send out letters to the target business's customers introducing the buyer as the new owner of the target business, and the seller fails to send out letters to some minor customers, the seller should not be able to claim that the obligation to send letters to all customers is now unenforceable. In other words, if a party does not enforce one provision of the Purchase Agreement, it does not act as a waiver relieving the other party from future obligations. This paragraph is necessary to allow each party the flexibility to determine which obligations to enforce and which to let go, without jeopardizing its right to enforce any provision of the Purchase Agreement in the future. This paragraph usually requires no negotiation.

(6) <u>Governing Law</u>: This paragraph chooses which state's (or country's) law will govern the interpretation of the Purchase Agreement and any disputes that might arise in connection with the deal. If the buyer, seller, and the

target business are all located in the same state, then you should choose that state's law. Sometimes people think that they should choose another state's law (e.g., Delaware) to govern the deal because it's trendy or might be more favorable to a certain party. Virginia courts will not apply the state law of a state to which neither the buyer, the seller, nor the target business has any relation, so choosing an unrelated state law probably is a waste of time and may create an additional dispute about which state's law applies.

If either the buyer, seller, or target business is in a different state, then the choice of governing law is negotiable. If the parties cannot agree on which state law to choose, I suggest choosing the state law of the state in which the target business is located. That probably will favor the buyer, but is reasonable because it will be the state law governing the business's operations.

(7) <u>Venue</u>: Venue refers to the location of a lawsuit. Interestingly, lawsuits about the deal can be brought in the federal or state courts sitting in one state, but require those courts to apply the law of a different state as a result of the state law chosen in the Governing Law paragraph. Choice of venue is strategic because a party may gain leverage in settlement negotiations if another party will need to travel to a different location to bring or defend a lawsuit. For example, if the buyer and target business are located in Virginia, but the seller is located in Florida because he retired there after closing, bringing a lawsuit in Virginia courts against the seller will put the seller at a disadvantage because he will have to travel to Virginia to defend the lawsuit. This will give the buyer more leverage during settlement negotiations because the seller will want to avoid travel costs.

Venue certainly is a negotiable issue, although it should not be a deal breaker. It seems reasonable that venue should be where the target business is located, but the seller or buyer might feel strongly about having the venue at its particular location. If we appear to be at an impasse on this issue, I usually suggest that the Venue paragraph indicate that venue will be in the buyer's location, if the seller brings the lawsuit against the buyer, and in the seller's location, if the buyer brings a lawsuit against the seller. This approach puts the risk of travel on the party bringing the lawsuit. This seems like a fair approach because it requires the party bringing the lawsuit to take into account the expenses of bringing a lawsuit in a different location. That factor might aid in motivating the parties to settle out of court.

(8) <u>Dispute Resolution</u>: Sometimes a Purchase Agreement will contain a provision detailing how disputes must be settled. Without a dispute resolution provision, each party is free to settle a dispute any way it wants to try, including suing the other party. That's a perfectly reasonable and acceptable approach.

A dispute resolution provision usually is included in a Purchase Agreement to require the parties to use an alternative dispute resolution process, such as negotiation, mediation, or arbitration. These provisions are customary and reasonable, although not necessary. If your Purchase Agreement contains a dispute resolution provision, make sure it spells out in clear detail what processes will be used, how to start the process, where you will meet, who will make the decisions, and whether the process is binding.

(9) <u>Assignment or No Assignment</u>: The parties, especially the seller, want to avoid the risk that they might end up

doing the deal with someone they don't know because one party transferred the Purchase Agreement to another party. Sometimes, the Purchase Agreement contains a paragraph prohibiting any transfer of the Purchase Agreement or rights (e.g., the right to receive the purchase price). Other times, the Purchase Agreement contains a paragraph that prohibits either party from assigning or transferring the Purchase Agreement or any of its rights (e.g., the right to receive the purchase price) to anyone else without the other party's prior written consent to the transfer.

In some instances, the buyer might have entered into the Purchase Agreement as an individual with the intention of forming a new company before the closing to take title to the assets. In that event, this paragraph should allow the buyer to assign the Purchase Agreement to his newly created company for that limited purpose. The seller might insist that the original buyer remain liable under the Purchase Agreement even after it has been assigned to the buyer's newly created company. The reasonableness of this request will depend on the circumstances, such as whether the newly created company will have adequate capital to operate and satisfy post-closing claims the seller might have against the buyer.

Prohibition of or restrictions on transferring the Purchase Agreement are reasonable but should reflect the reality of the parties' plans.

(10) <u>Successors and Assigns</u>: This paragraph is included to indicate clearly that if the Purchase Agreement is transferred to a new party, it will be binding and enforceable against that new party. This paragraph is reasonable and should not require any negotiation unless your business lawyer sees something wrong with the language in the paragraph.

(11) Notices: Certain provisions of the Purchase Agreement might require one party to notify another party for certain reasons, such as making a claim under the indemnification provision. Each party wants to avoid the risk of a situation where it loses its rights under the Purchase Agreement because it did not provide the other party with proper notice. Likewise, a party on whom a claim is made does not want to risk getting into a position where it fails to respond to a claim because it did not receive notice. Therefore, the Purchase Agreement will contain a Notice paragraph that indicates acceptable ways to give notice (e.g., by Certified Mail, Return Receipt Requested, overnight delivery that can be tracked, or fax), when notice will be deemed received, and to whom notice must be given (including all relevant address and contact information). Note that email notification typically is not an acceptable form of notice because it is too easy to claim that an email was never received or that it was overlooked. If you want email to be an acceptable form of notice, you should clearly indicate that in this paragraph, but also include conditions requiring return receipts or acknowledgments before the email notice is deemed effective. This paragraph is essential but typically does not require any negotiation.

(12) Headings: Each paragraph or section in the Purchase Agreement will have a heading, title, or name. There is a risk that the words in a paragraph or section will be inconsistent with the heading, title, or name. That inconsistency will make the meaning of the paragraph or section ambiguous. To avoid that risk, the Purchase Agreement usually contains a paragraph by which the parties agree that the headings, titles, and names of sections and

paragraphs will be disregarded when interpreting the Purchase Agreement.

(13) <u>Survival</u>: There is a principle in contract law that provides that once the Purchase Agreement has been fully performed at the closing, the Purchase Agreement is fulfilled. If that principle applies to your Purchase Agreement, it means any promises made in the Purchase Agreement for things that might occur after closing (e.g., indemnification) will be terminated. That's bad for both parties because most Purchase Agreements provide for some post-closing promises that flow to each party. To avoid the risk of having those post-closing promises terminated, the Purchase Agreement should contain a Survival paragraph that provides that the closing will not terminate the contract and that the representations, warranties, indemnities, and other promises and obligations contained in the Purchase Agreement will survive closing. Both parties should want this paragraph, but your business lawyer should look closely at its language to ensure it adequately addresses the risk.

(14) <u>Further Assurances</u>: You might discover after closing that you need a particular document drafted or signed to finish the deal. For example, you might discover a vehicle title that was inadvertently overlooked at closing and not signed, or you might discover that the web hosting service for the website you just bought requires that the seller work through an online process to transfer the domain name. Your Purchase Agreement may not have contemplated the need for the seller to do more things for you after closing to finish selling the business to you. A good Purchase Agreement will contain a catch-all paragraph by

which both parties agree to come back after closing to do additional things to transfer title to the buyer. This paragraph should require additional action only upon the reasonable request of the other party and if the other party pays the costs and expenses for the requested action. In other words, if the buyer needs an additional document drafted to transfer title to an asset, then the seller should not be required to pay for it.

(15) <u>Third-Party Beneficiaries:</u> When you see a paragraph in the Purchase Agreement with this heading, you should understand that it is there to prevent people who are not part of the deal from claiming they somehow should benefit from the deal. A good example of this would be a seller's creditor who makes a claim against the buyer for money because the buyer now owns the assets of the target business. This paragraph is an attempt to prevent that situation. It should appear in your Purchase Agreement, but probably will not need to be negotiated, unless your business lawyer discovers something odd about its language.

(16) <u>Attorney's Fee Shifting</u>: Under the American system, each party is required to pay its own attorney's fees in a dispute (e.g., arbitration or lawsuit), even if it wins, unless a statute or contract shifts that burden to the losing party. An Attorney's Fee Shifting paragraph should indicate that if one party brings a claim against the other, the losing party will pay the reasonable attorney's fees of the winning party. Having an Attorney's Fee Shifting paragraph in your Purchase Agreement also can motivate people to settle disputes without going to court because it causes people to second-guess the costs and risks of suing the other party. An Attorney's Fee Shifting paragraph also tends to level the playing field if one party has a lot more money

than the other party because it may keep the wealthier party from using a lawsuit for a weak claim as a way to run up the other party's attorney's fees and force them into a settlement.

Sometimes, buyers try to impose a unilateral obligation on a seller to pay the buyer's attorney's fees if the seller brings a lawsuit against the buyer and loses, or the seller might try to impose that unilateral obligation on the buyer. In either case, it is reasonable for either party to ask that the obligation be imposed on both parties.

If you want the Attorney's Fee Shifting paragraph to apply to different types of disputes, such as arbitration and settlements, you need to make sure the paragraph clearly says so; otherwise, it probably will not apply in those situations. In some states, the law may require that the contract clearly gives an arbitrator the right to award attorney's fees to the prevailing party, because of this, you probably want to include that authorization in your Purchase Agreement, too.

Finally, you don't want to give the other party a blank check for attorney's fees. For example, you do not want to create the risk that the seller engages the most expensive attorney in town for the dispute and you becoming responsible for paying those attorney's fees in the event you lose. Therefore, you should see that any reference to attorney's fees, costs, and expenses indicates that a party will be responsible for them in the event of a loss only if they are reasonable.

(17) <u>Counterparts</u>: In the past, closings were very formal. All parties sat at the same table and signed the same copy of the Purchase Agreement. As deals and technology have evolved, buyers and sellers frequently do not sit at the same table for closing (or even in the same city,

state, or country) or sign the same copy of the Purchase Agreement. Instead, they each have separate stacks of the deal documents that they sign at the location of their choice and convenience. These separate groups of deal documents are referred to as "counterparts." Signing counterparts result in signature pages for each deal document that contain only one party's signature—i.e., a set of signature pages with only the seller's signatures and a set of signatures with only the buyer's signatures.

The Purchase Agreement usually has a paragraph that allows this practice and indicates that the aggregate of all the signature pages will make up one enforceable Purchase Agreement. This is customary and usually should not require any negotiation, unless your business lawyer sees something unusual in the language.

(18) <u>Independent Legal Counsel</u>: This paragraph asks each party to agree that it was represented by its own lawyer, or, if it was not represented, that it had the right to be represented and chose not to be. This paragraph is especially important if you are dealing with a seller who decides it does not want to use a lawyer for the deal (usually to save on costs). In that situation, you do not want a seller to come back after closing and claim that you took advantage of them. You do not want to risk the possibility that an unrepresented seller could undo the deal. This paragraph is designed to prevent that risk.

Signature Block

The group of signatures at the end of the Purchase Agreement is referred to as the "signature block." You want to make sure that the right people are signing the Purchase Agreement. If you don't have the correct people signing the contract, you risk not being able to enforce the Purchase Agreement against the seller. For example, if the seller is a corporation, but the signature block requires only the founder of the corporation to sign in his personal capacity, then the corporation will not be obligated to perform under the Purchase Agreement because the corporation (through an authorized corporate officer) failed to sign the agreement.

Likewise, if the Purchase Agreement contains promises and obligations that the founder of the seller is to perform, such as a personal guaranty, the founder will not be obligated to perform if he has not signed the Purchase Agreement in his individual capacity. Your business lawyer should pay particular attention to see that the signature block includes the correct parties. Your business lawyer also should see that each person signing indicates his or her capacity and authority for signing. For example, if the seller is a corporation, the Purchase Agreement should require that the person signing on behalf of the corporation indicate his or her corporate title (e.g., President or Vice President). This seems like an inconsequential issue but could put a huge risk on you if the Purchase Agreement is not signed by the right people with the proper authority to bind the seller.

Paragraphs You Don't Need for a Simultaneous Closing

Above, I explained two different approaches to signing the Purchase Agreement and conducting the closing—i.e., signing the Purchase Agreement on one day, and then conducting closing at a later date or signing the Purchase Agreement and conducting closing on the same day. As a result of the differences in the timing of signing and closing, some provisions might not be needed in the Purchase Agreement—i.e., those provisions that apply to the time period between signing and closing.

For example, in a Purchase Agreement for a simultaneous closing, you probably don't need a provision that gives the buyer a due diligence period because there will not be a gap between signing and closing during which to conduct an investigation. You might also be able to forego some of the prerequisites for closing, such as the way in which the seller operates the business before closing.

Note, however, that if you take these provisions out of the Purchase Agreement, you should consider putting in additional representations and warranties to avoid the risks that bad things have happened before closing. For example, the Purchase Agreement should require that the seller represent and warrant to you that it has operated the target business in the ordinary course before closing, that inventory is at customary levels, and that it has not lost any significant customers or suppliers. Your business lawyer should be able to help you figure out which provision are not needed for a simultaneous closing and which representations and warranties to add.

In reality, however, most lawyers don't pay a lot of attention to the way in which a simultaneous closing impacts the Purchase Agreement. Instead, they simply use the same type of Purchase Agreement for either type of signing and closing. Make sure your business lawyer has reviewed the Purchase Agreement and determined that it adequately protects you and fits your deal.

Conclusion
You need to get the Purchase Agreement right. It is the linchpin to your entire deal. It allocates the risk appropriately between seller and buyer. If you mess it up, leave something out, or use ambiguous language, you might end up taking on risks that the seller

customarily should shoulder, or worse, risk having your deal undone. That's not the way to start your new business.

Any disagreement you have with the seller will be settled by looking at the Purchase Agreement. Get it wrong, and you probably will lose, or at least spend a lot of money trying to win (which also is a loss). Getting it right brings peace of mind as you transition into the target business smoothly.

The Purchase Agreement is not only the most important aspect of your deal but also the most complicated. I strongly recommend you get a business lawyer involved. Most people don't involve a business lawyer because they don't want to spend the money, but if you get a seasoned business lawyer, the money you spend on his fees will be a valuable investment. That investment can save you from big risks that will cost you much more when a problem arises later.

CHAPTER 12

WHAT HAPPENS BEFORE CLOSING?

Both the seller and you have a lot of work to do before closing, even though a Purchase Agreement has been signed. The seller's work is to make sure the target business is in good shape when title to the assets is transferred to you at closing. Your work is to make sure you have properly prepared yourself to own and run the business after closing. Each deal has its own type of unique circumstances, but below, I describe some of the more common items buyers and sellers need to address before closing.

Seller's Pre-Closing Work

Operate in the Ordinary Course
The seller should have promised in the Purchase Agreement that it will operate the business "in the ordinary course" before closing. This means the seller needs to run the target business as it always has, up to the closing date. The seller needs to continue to advertise and market the business, seek out new customers, process orders, make products, and do all the other things it normally

does or should be doing, to run the business as if it were not going to be sold. The seller also needs to maintain its existing customer base by taking care of its customers, resolving disputes, processing refunds, and serving each customer quickly and reasonably. If the seller loses a big customer before closing, the buyer might be able to call off the deal because the target business will have lost a lot of value.

Maintain Inventory
If the target business has an inventory of supplies or products, the seller should have promised in the Purchase Agreement that it will have adequate inventory on hand at the closing. For example, if the target business is a healthcare practice, the seller needs to make sure the practice has an adequate amount of medical supplies on hand at the closing in order for the buyer to open the practice the next day and treat patients. If the seller is a retail store, the shelves need to be adequately stocked with products at closing so the buyer can open the store the next day and have enough product on hand to serve its customers. This is a big deal to the buyer because not having enough inventory will hurt the business at a critical time. If the seller does not have enough inventory on hand, then the buyer will incur the cost of buying needed inventory and waiting for that inventory to be delivered shortly after closing. The buyer will lose business during that waiting period. Some customers may never return because they have lost faith in the business, so this harm can impact the buyer long after it obtains enough inventory.

Help Obtain Consents
The seller should work cooperatively with the buyer to obtain any required consents to transfer the purchased assets. For example,

if the buyer is assuming the lease and needs the landlord's consent for that to happen, the seller should be the one to contact the landlord first to introduce the buyer and notify the landlord about the upcoming deal. It would be awkward if the buyer contacted the landlord seemingly out of the blue to get that consent. Likewise, the seller should be the first to contact any other customers, vendors, or suppliers who need to consent to the deal. The seller should introduce the buyer and also provide any information the landlord, customer, vendor, or supplier needs to give its permission to transfer a lease or contract to the buyer.

If the seller does not cooperate, closing might be delayed, which could hurt the seller if it is trying to close soon to pay off creditors, move into retirement, stop the bleeding of a declining business, or any other reason for which the seller wants a quick exit. Ultimately, if the required consents are not obtained, the buyer could terminate the deal.

Help with Employees
The buyer might also ask the seller to help persuade key employees to stay on after closing. Likewise, the buyer might ask the seller to help with delivering the message to other employees that they will not be offered jobs after closing. This is a delicate issue because you want to avoid a situation where employees leave the business as soon as they find out about the sale. Their exit could seriously harm the business before closing if the business is left short-staffed. The seller should know each employee, and, as a result, be able to suggest a strategy to the buyer for approaching each employee. The seller will need not only to introduce the buyer to the employees but also "sell" the employees on the buyer as the new owner.

Remove Excluded Assets

Finally, if the Purchase Agreement allows the seller to keep certain assets (the "Excluded Assets"), then before closing is the time for the seller to remove them from the business. You may not want the seller to return to the business after closing to pick up the Excluded Assets if you believe his presence might be somewhat disruptive to your takeover.

The Lingering Seller

> Cheryl is a doctor who purchased an existing practice. After closing, the seller kept visiting the practice. During his visits, he would disrupt employees, poke around the practice, look at files, and interact with patients. His visits hijacked Cheryl's attention because she needed not only to attend to her patients and staff but also to the seller and his disruptions. In addition, Cheryl decided to terminate certain staff and hire new employees shortly after closing. This change upset the seller, and he voiced his opinion about the buyer's decision while in the office in front of staff and patients. Cheryl ended up having to have an uncomfortable contentious conversation with the seller and to change the locks on the office. This incident transpired over a three-month period after closing, which was a critical time for Cheryl to focus on spinning up her new practice.

Be careful that the seller does not remove anything you need to operate the business after closing. If the Purchase Agreement allows the seller to keep his laptop, but the laptop contains the business's accounting system, then you will want to make sure you get a copy of the accounting data and the business's financial data before he removes the laptop. You probably should have him delete the accounting data from the laptop after you have installed it on your computer, after closing.

Bulk Sales Act Compliance
If you and the seller have not waived the applicability of the Bulk Sales Act, then the seller needs to spend the time before closing notifying creditors and taking the other necessary steps to comply with that law. The Bulk Sales Act will have timelines and deadlines that must be met before closing. The seller needs to start its Bulk Sales Act Compliance far enough before closing to allow time to comply.

Buyer's Pre-Closing Work

Set Up Acquisition Entity
You probably will need a new corporation or limited liability company to take title to the purchased assets. Your business lawyer and CPA can advise you on what to do. If you decide to form a new entity, the time for setting it up is before closing.

In many states, you can set up an entity very quickly; I can set one up in Virginia in about an hour. You may be tempted to wait until just before closing to form your entity, but that might be a mistake. If you are getting a loan to finance the purchase, you want the loan to be made to your entity, not you personally, even though you likely will be required to personally guarantee the loan. If you wait until the last minute to set up your acquisition entity, it might be too late for the bank to change the loan and put it in the name of your entity. Tell your lender at the beginning of the loan process that you will be setting up a new entity, and that you want the entity to be the borrower. Then set up the entity as soon as possible to avoid a situation where the lender will no longer allow a change in the loan documents.

If there will be multiple owners of the acquisition entity, you probably need some time before closing to negotiate the terms of their ownership, especially if some of the owners will not be involved in the business, (i.e., passive investors). Avoid the risk of holding up or postponing closing because the details of your owners have not been ironed out. This is another reason to create your acquisition entity as soon as possible before closing.

Conduct Due Diligence
The Purchase Agreement should give you a limited amount of time after signing to investigate the target business thoroughly. Begin investigation as soon as the Purchase Agreement is signed. Conduct the investigation as quickly as possible so that you will have time before the Due Diligence Period ends to decide whether to terminate the deal or move forward.

Obtain Financing
If you need to borrow money to pay all or part of the Purchase Price, secure that financing as soon as you can before closing. The Purchase Agreement should give you a limited time period after signing the Purchase Agreement to obtain a binding loan commitment from a lender of your choice. Ideally, you already are having preliminary, informal discussions with one or more potential lenders before signing the Purchase Agreement. As soon as the

Purchase Agreement has been signed, press the potential lenders for a loan commitment so that you have adequate time to determine whether you can obtain a loan on acceptable terms or terminate the deal.

Obtain Consents
If you are taking over a lease or other contracts from the seller, and the transfer of those contracts requires the landlord or other contracting party to give permission to the transfer, then you need to obtain that permission before closing. In my experience, the most common reason for postponing closing is the need for more time to obtain these consents. That delay usually occurs because giving consent is not a high priority and sometimes a perceived nuisance for the landlord or other contracting party. As a result, the landlord or other contracting party usually puts the consent at the bottom of its to-do list. This means that the seller and you need to contact the landlord or other contracting parties as soon as possible to get this process started.

Another reason for contacting the landlord or other contracting party as soon as possible to request the required consent is that the landlord or other contracting party might require that you provide it with certain information for review before they will consent to the transfer. Many landlords will want to see your financial statements to determine whether you are a good credit risk before agreeing to transfer the lease to you. They also may want information about the individual owners of the buyer to assess their individual credit worthiness. This is customary and reasonable, but you will need time to gather and deliver that information, and the landlord or other contracting party will need time to review the information.

Obtain Licenses, Permits, or Government Permissions

If you need licenses, permits, or other government permission to acquire or operate the target business, and can obtain it before closing, now is the time to do so. For example, if you need to get a business license from your local government, do it before closing. If you need to take a test to obtain a contractor's license or some other type of ratification or license, take the test before closing.

Obtain Insurance

You will need insurance to protect your business after closing. You will need to figure out what type and how much insurance is needed (often referred to as the "limits"). If you are borrowing money from a commercial lender, the lender will dictate the type and amount of insurance required. If you are not borrowing money, consider obtaining commercial general liability with any additional riders to cover unique aspects of the business.

Consult with an insurance agent as soon as possible after signing the Purchase Agreement. Share your lender's insurance requirements with the agent, if you are borrowing money for the purchase. If no lender is involved, provide the agent with information about the target business, including the purchase price, and the business's financial history. The agent should be able to answer questions about the type and amount of insurance to consider. The agent should provide quotes for the recommended insurance.

Line Up Employees

The period between signing and closing is the time to consider what to do with the seller's employees. Will you keep all of the employees on after closing? Will you terminate some employees on the closing date? How will you make offers to the employees you want to keep? How will you work with the seller and its employees to set up your employment situation without alienating the employees you won't keep, risking that they will quit and hurt the target business before closing? Work closely with the seller to answer these questions before closing and before approaching the employees.

Once the seller and you have worked out a strategy, consider approaching employees to make your employment offers. This is especially important for key employees that will be given a written employment agreement. You will want time before closing to work out the terms of those employment agreements. Eliminate the risk that a key employee will "walk" after closing by settling the terms of the employment agreement before closing.

Resist the temptation to sit back and wait for closing after you sign the Purchase Agreement. The period after signing the Purchase Agreement is the time to determine whether you will terminate the deal during the due diligence period. Your efforts to resolve issues before closing will help you get to closing on time, decrease your frustration level, and help you transition smoothly into the new business after closing.

CHAPTER 13

THE CLOSING

The day has finally arrived for you to take ownership of the target business. You have done your due diligence, set up your acquisition entity, obtained your financing, obtained the consents you need to take on leases and contracts, made your offers to employees you want to keep, and finished all your other pre-closing tasks. Now you need to sign and exchange documents with the seller and pay the purchase price: this is closing.

Formal Versus Informal

When I started practicing law 25 years ago, closings were very formal. By formal, I mean both parties and their lawyers would sit down at the same table in a lawyer's office and proceed through a ceremony where each document would be presented, briefly explained, and then signed by all the parties. At the conclusion of the closing, the seller and buyer each would walk away with a stack of signed original documents that completed the asset purchase. Formal closings took a lot of time and required that each party and its lawyer be able to coordinate their schedules to attend the closing.

Formal closings are not as common today. Technology makes it much easier for the parties to close the deal without sitting at the same table. Formal closings are still useful, however, in certain circumstances. Sometimes, the buyer and seller just want to sit down together and get the closing finished as quickly as possible. Other times, the buyer and seller might need to negotiate issues that are still open. In those instances, it makes sense to conduct a formal closing with everyone present at the same time.

Most small business purchases are closed using an informal process. The buyer and seller usually agree on a day for transferring title to the assets. That decision might be driven by any number of factors, including, but not limited to, how fast the buyer can get its bank financing and how quickly the buyer and seller can get consents to transfer a lease and other contracts. The buyer and seller also might pick a closing date that coincides with the beginning or end of a month in order to simplify the pro-rated expenses allocated to each party. There may be other business factors unique to the target business that drive the decision of when to schedule closing. For example, I recently helped a client sell a retail business that sells seasonal clothing. The buyer and seller wanted to schedule closing before the beginning of the season to give the buyer the advantage of owning the target business for the full season.

When the closing date arrives, each party usually meets with its business lawyer at the lawyer's office. The lawyer has printed up copies of all of the finalized documents for closing. You will sit with your lawyer and sign each of the closing documents. These signed copies are some of the counterparts explained in Chapter 11. The copies the seller signs at closing also are counterparts.

After you leave your lawyer's office, she will exchange copies of the signed closing documents with the seller's attorney. The method of exchanging signed documents should be agreed upon by the lawyers before closing. Some methods of delivering signed documents include: scanning and emailing the documents on the closing date and delivering the originals by hand, overnight delivery, or mail a few days later; exchanging copies of the signature pages (either by email or fax) and delivering original, signed documents shortly after closing; or exchanging signed originals by hand delivery on the closing date.

If you are borrowing money from a bank or other commercial lender, then your business lawyer will send the bank copies of the signed loan documents. The lender will then fund the loan by wiring the loan proceeds to your business lawyer's trust account. In some instances, the lender may issue a certified check for the loan proceeds, instead of a wire transfer. The lender will rely on your business lawyer to disburse the loan proceeds in accordance with the loan documents.

Regardless of whether you have a formal or informal closing, always feel free to ask your lawyer any questions about the deal or the closing. You should already have read over all the closing documents because your lawyer should have shared them with you before you reached her office. If you have not had the chance to review a document before the closing, ask for some time to do so at your lawyer's office. Ask your lawyer any questions about the closing documents before you sign them. My practice is to give a brief explanation of each closing document before they are signed and to ask whether my client has any questions. No lawyer wants a client to come back after closing upset about the contents of a closing document because he didn't read or understand it before signing.

Closing Documents

There are several documents for the seller and you to sign at closing. Many times, buyers cannot understand why so many documents are necessary, but you should understand that the documents signed at closing are designed to transfer title to the assets and make sure the parties are keeping all of their promises to each other.

The parties might also wonder why a lot of the agreements contained in the documents don't appear in one document. Agreements appear in separate documents for at least two reasons. First, to avoid the possibility of having one document containing many agreements being ruled unenforceable. In that instance, the invalidity of the document risks nullifying all the agreements contained in the document. Lawyers put separate agreements in separate documents to avoid this risk. Second, some documents might need to be disclosed or turned over to other parties, such as government agencies and lenders. By putting each agreement in a separate document, you avoid disclosing all the terms of the deal when you have to turn over a particular document.

None of the documents presented at closing should come as a surprise because the business lawyer, seller's lawyer, you, and the seller should have been involved in drafting and negotiating those documents before closing. You should have received copies of those drafts for your review and input before closing. You also should have had the chance to ask your business lawyer any questions about the closing documents, or even for a brief explanation of what they are and why they are necessary, before closing.

Here are some of the more common documents that get signed at closing:

(1) <u>Closing Checklist</u>—I share a checklist with my client as a reference to help my client understand what I am doing, what she needs to do, and what to expect at closing. It's like the table of contents for the entire deal. This is simply a document to have as a good practice. I usually create a checklist early on in a deal containing the pre-closing, closing, and post-closing items that need to happen and all the documents that will be required to close the deal. I use the checklist as a project management tool to get us to closing. I also use it to run my closing to make sure we have not forgotten anything. No one signs the closing checklist.

(2) <u>Asset Purchase Agreement</u>—If the Purchase Agreement was not signed earlier, it should be the first document signed at closing. This is the legal document that controls the entire transaction, so it needs to be signed by both parties, or you will not have a deal. I know verbal agreements are enforceable in my state, but they are difficult and expensive to prove, especially when the other party to the deal will have different perceptions and positions on the terms of the deal.

(3) <u>Side Agreements</u>—Side agreements are separate, short written amendments to the Purchase Agreement to address specific issues that were identified and resolved shortly before or at closing. For example, at the closing, the seller might ask to keep a business computer. If the buyer agrees, their lawyers should draft a brief letter memorializing that change to the deal.

(4) <u>Bill of Sale</u>—Most assets you are buying do not have a document that indicates who owns it. Real estate has a deed, vehicles have titles, but most other assets have no written title document associated with them. The business

lawyers will draft a Bill of Sale as the document that transfers title to assets that do not already have a title document. The Bill of Sale acts like a deed or a vehicle title for those assets.

This document usually does not need to be negotiated, but your business lawyer should make sure that it incorporates the terms of the Purchase Agreement, including any representations and warranties the seller has made about the purchased assets. Doing this will help eliminate the risk of a dispute where the seller claims that the Bill of Sale somehow negates any representations and warranties made in the Purchase Agreement.

(5) <u>Vehicle or Equipment Titles</u>—Some of the assets you are buying might have their own title documents (e.g., vehicles, trailers, and heavy equipment). The seller should sign and deliver all of these titles over to you at closing so you can take them to your motor vehicle administration as soon as possible after closing to get the titles changed into your name. If the seller has loans on these assets, the loans will have to be paid off first out of the purchase proceeds in order for the lender to release the titles. The lender will sign the titles to indicate the liens have been released. Then you will need to get the seller to sign them so title can be transferred to you.

(6) <u>Secretary's Certificate</u>—This is a document from an officer of the seller or buyer entity that certifies that the person signing the closing documents on behalf of the entity is authorized to bind the entity. Most asset purchases I handle do not require a Secretary's Certificate anymore, but it's not a big deal if you are asked to provide one for closing. Of course, if you have to provide a Secretary's Certificate, you should insist that the seller also provides one.

(7) <u>Bring-Down Certificate</u>—If you signed the Purchase Agreement before closing, and the buyer and seller each made representations and warranties to each other in the Purchase Agreement, there will be a gap between the time the Purchase Agreement was signed and the closing. Each party will want to make sure that the representations and warranties made by the other party when the Purchase Agreement was signed are still true at closing. The Bring-Down Certificate handles that issue by requiring each party to promise to the other party that its representations and warranties are still true at closing. Each party should sign and deliver a Bring-Down Certificate to the other party at closing.

(8) <u>Assignment and Assumption of Lease</u>—If you are taking over the seller's lease, then there should be a separate document to be signed at closing by which the seller assigns the lease to you, and you assume responsibility for it. Sometimes, that document also is signed by the landlord to show its consent to the lease transfer. One reason to have this separate document is to avoid the risk of having to disclose a copy of the Purchase Agreement to the landlord. This agreement is customary and reasonable. It should refer to the Purchase Agreement. It probably will not require any negotiation, unless your business lawyer notices that something is missing from the document or that the document contains some unusual language.

(9) <u>Assignment and Assumption of Other Contracts</u>—If you are taking over other contracts from the seller, there should be a separate document to be signed at closing by which the seller assigns those contracts to you and you assume responsibility for them. Sometimes, that document also is signed by the other parties to the contracts to show

their consent to the transfer. One reason to have this separate document is to avoid the risk of having to disclose a copy of the Purchase Agreement to the other parties of the transferred contracts. This agreement is customary and reasonable. It should refer to the Purchase Agreement. It probably will not require any negotiation, unless your business lawyer notices that something is missing from the document or that the document contains some unusual language.

(10) <u>Assignment of Patents, Trademarks, Copyrights, and Other Intellectual Property Rights</u>—If you are buying patents, trademarks, copyrights, trade secrets, or other intellectual property rights from the seller, then you should have a separate document that assigns those rights to your acquisition entity. There are at least two reasons for having this document. First, the law requires that the assignment of some of these intellectual property rights be done by using specific words and phrases for the transfer to be valid and enforceable. Second, the law also may require that the transfer document be recorded in the public records of a governmental agency (e.g., the U.S. Patent & Trademark Office or the U.S. Copyright Office) for it to be valid and enforceable. Because you do not want to put the entire Purchase Agreement into the public record to be available for all to see, only this separate assignment document is recorded. Your business lawyer should ensure that this assignment document contains the language required by law to be enforceable, valid, and recordable.

(11) <u>Settlement Statement</u>—This is a short document that shows how the purchase price will be paid in and disbursed. Most small business deals do not use a Settlement Statement unless the seller has debts or other expenses

(e.g., prorated taxes, utilities, etc.) that need to be paid out of the purchase price to avoid the risk of the buyer becoming liable for those debts or expenses. In that instance, it is reasonable for the parties to agree in writing how the purchase price will be disbursed before the balance will be paid over to the seller. Both parties should sign the Settlement Statement at closing to indicate their agreement with the proposed disbursements.

(12) <u>Escrow Agreement</u>—If the Purchase Agreement requires that some of the purchase price is to be put in escrow for a period after closing, then the buyer and seller should sign an Escrow Agreement that appoints an escrow agent (usually either the buyer's or seller's business lawyer) and describes in detail the circumstances under which the money can be disbursed. Pay particular attention to the circumstances that will trigger disbursement of the escrow to ensure that they are clearly defined and meet with your understanding of which party will shoulder the risk for certain expenses and losses. This document should be signed by the buyer, seller, and escrow agent.

(13) <u>Promissory Note</u>—If the seller is allowing you to defer payments of the purchase price, you will need to sign and deliver a promissory note to the seller at the closing. The Note will contain the terms of the loan, including the interest rate, the amount of time you will have to pay off the loan, and the frequency and amounts of the installment payments. This document will have been negotiated in detail before closing. You should sign and deliver only one original of the Promissory Note to avoid the risk of paying off the Note, having it canceled, and then having another original, signed copy show up afterward with a claim that it hasn't been paid in full.

(14) Security Agreement—If the seller is allowing you to defer part of the purchase price with a promissory note, then the seller probably will also require that you pledge the purchased assets as collateral to secure the payment of the promissory note. In that instance, you will sign a Security Agreement at closing to make that pledge and to create a lien on the purchased assets that the seller can exercise to foreclose on the assets if you fail to pay the promissory note.

(15) Personal Guaranty—If the seller is allowing you to defer part of the purchase price with a promissory note, then the seller probably will also require that you, the other owners of the acquisition entity, and perhaps even your spouse guarantee to pay the promissory note personally, if the acquisition entity fails to pay the note. Each individual guaranteeing the promissory note will need to sign and deliver a separate personal guaranty document at closing.

(16) Bank Loan Documents—If you are getting a loan from a bank or other commercial lender to finance part of the purchase price, your lender will have sent all the loan documents to your business lawyer shortly before closing. These documents usually consist of a loan agreement, promissory note, security agreement, personal guaranty, agreement to obtain and maintain insurance on the purchased assets, and other documents meant to obligate you to pay the loan and to allow the lender to foreclose on the business if you fail to pay. Your business lawyer will walk you through signing all of these loan documents as part of the closing. Your lawyer will then deliver these documents to the lender so that the lender will fund the loan. The lender's loan documents usually are not

negotiable because the lender needs its documents to be consistent so that it can sell them on a secondary market. Nevertheless, you and your business lawyer should review the loan documents before closing to make sure that they contain the terms (e.g., interest rate, payment term, payment amounts, and payment frequency) set forth in the loan commitment and to ensure that the documents do not contain any unusual terms.

Keys, Passwords, Alarm Codes

Closing usually is focused on big items, like getting documents signed, financing loans, and paying the purchase price. But you also want to make sure you have whatever little things you need to open and run the business the day after closing. You will need keys to all doors, codes and passcards for security systems, and passwords for networks, software, web hosting applications, and cloud-based applications. I suggest you put these items on your closing checklist and have the seller collect these before closing so they can be turned over at closing. By having everything turned over at closing, you will avoid the risk of the seller keeping control of anything you purchase, having to chase the seller down to get these items after closing, or risking the possibility of the seller trying to hold these items hostage after closing. Should a "hostage" situation arise, it might cost less to pay off the seller for his unfounded demand, rather than fight him in court. If you prepare before closing, however, you can avoid these risks.

Purchase Price Payment and Disbursement

As the buyer, you also will pay the purchase price. The purchase price might take the form of a certified check made payable to the buyer's lawyer or the seller, or you might wire the purchase price into your lawyer's trust account.

The method for delivering the purchase should be agreed upon before closing. For example, if a check to pay the purchase price is made payable to the seller, then the lawyers may agree that the buyer's lawyer will deliver the check to the seller or the seller's lawyer.

If the seller needs to pay off debts and other expenses out of the purchase price, then the purchase price should not be delivered directly to the seller. Doing so would risk a situation where the seller is tempted to keep all the money and not pay off its creditors.

The Surfer Seller

Brodie was selling his pizza restaurant. He was about 24 years old and had a number of debts to pay with the purchase price, including his attorney's fees. Unfortunately, his attorney had the purchase price delivered directly to Brodie. As soon as Brodie received the check for the purchase price, he took a trip to Costa Rica to go surfing. He spent all the money on his surfing trip, rather than paying off his creditors and attorney's fees.

If this situation were to happen in your deal, you might be left to deal with the seller's creditors.

If the purchase price is to be used to pay off creditors and other obligations, then the lawyers should agree before the closing on how that is to happen. Typically, this agreement will appear in the Settlement Statement. One lawyer should be responsible for receiving and disbursing the purchase price to the seller's creditors shortly after all closing documents have been signed and exchanged. Only after the buyer's lawyer is satisfied that the seller's creditors have been paid should the lawyer responsible for disbursing the purchase price pay over the balance to the seller.

Time Requirements

The actual document signing portion of the closing usually doesn't take very long. You might be at the closing for about an hour. The lawyers will then need some time to exchange documents, obtain loan proceeds, disburse the purchase price, and send the signed closing documents to their clients. Those activities don't impact your time, but you should be aware that the lawyers will need to do more work and need additional time after you sign the closing documents.

In addition, you also should consider setting aside time to get together with the seller shortly after both of you have signed the closing documents. This time might be spent handing off keys and making your initial transition into your new business. You might even need to start operating the business immediately. Also, you will want to start working on your post-closing items as soon as possible.

CHAPTER 14

WHAT YOU NEED TO DO AFTER CLOSING

Closing is finished. You have signed all the documents, obtained your financing, and paid the purchase price. The seller has transferred title to the purchased assets to you. You own the business. Do you feel like the deal is done? There are a few things you need to take care of after closing to finish your transition into the new business. Your business lawyer needs to help you with some of these items because they are legal issues. Others, you will need to do yourself. Getting these things done as soon as possible after closing will put you in full control of the business.

Training

The period for receiving whatever transition assistance you negotiated with the seller should take place after closing. The transition might consist of a hand-off meeting with the seller where he gives you pertinent information, walks you around the facility, and turns over what is needed to run the business. It might take just a few hours, or, if you bargained for it, the seller might be required to train you and your management team on how to run the business. You should receive that training as soon as possible after closing.

The more time you wait after closing, the more difficult it might be to get the seller's help because the seller will become disinterested and disengaged and may have moved on to other interests.

Transition of Customers, Vendors, and Suppliers

Contact customers, vendors, and suppliers as soon as possible after closing to let them know that you now own the business. If the purchased business is to have a chance at success under your new ownership, you need to keep as many of these relationships as possible because they will be the lifeblood and cash flow of the business. It's typically easier and less expensive to keep a customer than it is to find a new customer.

Sometimes, this contact consists of introduction letters. Those letters might come from you or the seller, depending on what was negotiated into your deal. Either way, those letters need to go out right after closing. You also might decide to contact customers, vendors, and suppliers directly by visiting their offices or calling them on the phone. Site visits can be a powerful way to retain relationships, especially with customers.

If the seller promised in the Purchase Agreement to help you with these efforts, you need to engage the seller shortly after closing. Again, the longer you wait to get the seller's help with customer, vendor, and supplier transition, the less chance you will have for an enthusiastic seller who will help you retain these critical relationships.

Switching Over Utilities and Domain Name

You cannot switch over the utilities to your new business (e.g., phones, internet service, electric, gas, and water and sewer) until after you own the business. There may be other services, too, such as uniform service or hazardous waste disposal service, which cannot be switched over until after you actually own the business. You probably will be required to pay security deposits when you switch utilities and other services because the service provider will refund the seller's deposits. While switching over utilities and other services is not critical to the business, it will make the administration of these accounts easier if they are in the name of your new business as soon as possible after closing.

If you purchased a domain name from the seller, you will need to work with the seller to get the domain name transferred to your new business. Most website hosting services have a well-defined process for making that transfer. The transfer can be done online. The transfer process usually requires that the seller initiate it and fill out and submit the required form online.

Your business lawyer should be able to tell you how to complete the transfer process. While doing so is not complicated, many times it takes some effort to discover the process because it is not prominently featured on the web host's website.

You need to get this transfer done shortly after closing. Otherwise, the seller will continue to control your website, which could be critical if you take customer orders through the site. There might be a small fee involved in transferring the domain name, which you will be required to pay unless the seller agreed in the Purchase Agreement to pay it.

Recording Title Documents

Title documents for any purchased assets need to be recorded immediately after closing. Examples of title documents to record include vehicle titles, patent assignments, trademark assignments, and copyright assignments. Your lawyer should take care of the recording, if possible. He likely will not be able to record vehicle titles, however, because, as the new owner, you will need to visit your local motor vehicle administration to handle that.

Each title document recordation probably will require a small fee. You will be responsible for paying that fee unless the seller agreed in the Purchase Agreement to pay it.

Record vehicle titles as soon as possible after closing for insurance purposes. The timing for recording the other title documents might not be as critical, but still should be done relatively soon after closing.

Recording Liens

If you obtained any financing for the purchase price, whether from the seller or a lender, that financing probably is secured by a lien on the purchased assets. The lender will want to protect that lien by recording a Uniform Commercial Code Financing Statement, usually referred to as a "UCC-1." This may be handled by your business lawyer, the seller's lawyer, or the lender. Regardless of who handles the recording, it should be done shortly after closing to preserve the lender's rights in the collateral. In some states, recording can be done online. A filing fee is charged for recording each lien, which you will be required to pay.

Obtaining Licenses, Permits, or other Government Approval

Some licenses and permits to operate a business cannot be obtained until you own the business. For example, in Virginia, you cannot obtain an alcoholic beverage control license for a restaurant, bar, or club until you own that business. You need to get those licenses immediately after closing so you can operate the business without interruption.

Public Announcement

Because you now own the business, you have total control over making public announcements about your new ownership, unless, for some odd reason, you have agreed in the Purchase Agreement not to do so, or to do so only with the seller's permission. A post-closing restriction on your ability to announce the new ownership would be abnormal, though. You should be very careful, however, not to disparage or criticize the seller in any of your advertising, marketing, or announcements. If you have questions about the content of your public announcements, you should ask for your business lawyer's advice.

If you want to hang a banner, send out a direct mailer, mount an email campaign, issue a press release, broadcast radio or television commercials, or make any other public announcement that you now own the purchased business, you should consider doing so shortly after closing. You will be responsible for paying whatever costs are associated with these marketing and announcement efforts.

Earn-Out

If you agreed to pay the seller an "earn-out," which usually is a percentage of your profits after closing based on the business's performance, then you need to remain aware of the formula for calculating the earn out and the timeline for paying it. Taking care of the earn-out after closing will be your responsibility. If you fail to pay, or are late on paying the earn-out, the seller may become agitated. Dealing with an unhappy seller after closing will take your focus away from operating your new business at a critical time, which may hurt your new business. You should get your business lawyer's advice on any questions about how to calculate or pay the earn-out.

Most of these post-closing items can be completed within a few weeks after closing, while a few, such as the earn-out, may take longer. Sellers have all kinds of reactions to no longer being the business owner: some disappear; they may become uncooperative; others are so happy they might not want to be engaged in the business anymore, even in transition; and still others just can't seem to let go and act as if they still own the business. Regardless of the seller's reaction, you probably will benefit from distancing yourself from the seller. The sooner you finish these post-closing tasks, the sooner you can disengage your relationship with the seller and move on independently as the new owner of the business.

CHAPTER 15

THE DEAL IS DONE

At the end of the closing, I shake my client's hand and wish them good luck in the business. My client usually is pretty happy at that point.

Other than some post-closing items, my work on the deal is done. I usually don't see my client again, until they are ready to do another deal. It's a tidy ending to a process we have been working on for many months.

Now that you have finished reading this book, you are an educated business buyer. You understand that buying a business is a process, not an event. You understand the entire process. You won't be surprised during the deal and are better prepared to operate the business as soon as you step into it after closing. Because of your knowledge of the deal process, you may also have a better relationship with your business lawyer and save on legal fees.

If you work with your team and follow the suggestions contained in this book, your process should go smoothly. You should have crafted your deal in a way that reduced your risks as much as reasonably possible. As a result, you should be able to operate the business after closing without concern for any additional legal problems relating to the deal.

You will have questions throughout the deal process. This book is your starting point. Your team members are there to provide specific answers, guidance, and advice.

Good luck with your new business!